HOW TO CREATE YOUR
GIGPO
BAND T-
ALBUM COVERS

Screenprinting, Photocopy Art, Mixed-Media Collage,

OWN

POSTERS

SHIRTS, & STICKERS

and Other Guerilla Poster Styles

RUTHANN GODOLLEI

Voyageur Press

Acknowledgments

Thanks to the Dregnis, Jenski, CBU, KASJ & SH, Rita Nadir, Juani, Wiggly Science,
Wet Paint, Macalester College, TCTCC, Chris of the VRC, Larry Liu, Thursday Lunch Mel,
Yaz, KK, ZZ, and friends of Printland.

First published in 2013 by Voyageur Press, an imprint of
MBI Publishing Company, 400 First Avenue North, Suite 300,
Minneapolis, MN, 55401 USA

MBI Publishing Company titles are also available at discounts in
bulk quantity for industrial or sales-promotional use. For details
write to Special Sales Manager at MBI Publishing Company, 400
First Avenue North, Suite 300, Minneapolis, MN, 55401 USA.

ISBN: 978-0-7603-4314-2

Library of Congress Cataloging-in-Publication Data

Godollei, Ruthann.
  How to create your own gig posters, band T-shirts, album covers &
stickers : screenprinting, photocopy
art, mixed-media collage, and other
guerilla poster styles / by Ruthann
Godollei.
     pages cm
  Includes index.
  ISBN 978-0-7603-4314-2 (sc)
  1. Printing--Technique. I. Title.
  NE860.G57 2013
  760.28--dc23

2012030692

Editor: Dennis Pernu
Design manager: James Kegley
Cover fonts: Chank Diesel
Book designer: Simon Larkin
Layout: Chris Fayers

Printed in China

CONTENTS

Introduction		6
1	Stencils	8
2	Linocuts and Woodcuts	26
3	Digital Printing and Photocopies	56
4	Screenprinting	80
5	Stamping	110
6	Now That You Have the Printing Bug . . .	130
Resources		155
Index		158

I have lost count of the number of posters, fliers, stickers, record and CD covers, T-shirts, and ephemera I've printed, taught students to make, and helped fledgling bands print. Besides the monetary savings, the pride in being able to make your own is so satisfying. A sign in my print shop reads, "The power of the press belongs to those who can operate one."

In an era of mass production, few people retain the knowledge or skills to print for themselves. This book will provide basic hands-on printing practices for those with little or no experience, and it may give experienced printers some quick-and-dirty alternatives to high-end equipment and processes.

practical terms, they communicate useful information and hopefully do it in a graphically effective way. They give visual cues about aural experiences. And consider the print's contribution to the observed environment. Are blank walls and phone poles really aesthetically pleasing? Hand-printed items retain a unique look with which no mass-produced objects can compete. They have your personal aesthetics as well as the flaws and happy accidents that make hand printing so one-of-a-kind yet still part of a set. You can just tell they're made by human beings.

And why make multiples? Obviously so more people can see your gig, receive a message, or get your music in a cool container. But also consider the survival factor. If you

Introduction

I always tell my students that, like martial arts schools, printmaking teachers have their preferred styles and secret ninja techniques. There are a lot of ways to go about getting a print. I have tried to make this guide relatively simple, inexpensive, and, above all, doable with things a normal person might have access to. If a taste of DIY printing gets you interested in learning more, great—there are lots of books, online resources, schools, and professionals you can consult.

In making a case for offering this information in book form, I might point out that if the electrical power goes out you can still access this reference. And many of the printing techniques in this book will require no electricity. Paper still is a renewable resource. And it is not pay-per-view.

Why make printed objects in a world of online and virtual notification? Poke through a stack of old prints, magazines, band posters, or advertising illustrations in a secondhand store and you'll see they not only provided the information the users at the time needed, but they also give us a record of their day. Prints are records of events enjoyed, bands that were "in," places where culture happened, social concerns, and communities—in short, visual culture. In

are postering today and some get torn down or nabbed as collector items (and isn't that a high compliment?), the more you print the greater the chances that at least a few will stay up. In addition, history shows that an object in multiple has a chance of surviving, somewhere, if only because someone thought it was interesting and kept it.

Each print process covered here has its own aesthetic look, its own strong points and drawbacks, things it is good for and things it really isn't. You might want to read over a particular process and see if you have access to the materials needed first. Also, look at the featured artists and exemplars and see if that is the look or visual effect you're after. The main things you really need in order to print are a good idea, the willingness to try, a disregard for getting dirty, and your own human labor.

Opposite: This print is part of a graphic novel done entirely in woodcut prints. The artist lets the grain of the wood add texture to the design. *Down Is the New Up*, in which a group of ghosts take over a letterpress shop, can be seen at the artist's website. Don't worry: your adventures in printing won't be as dreary as it is for these haunting fellows. *Artist: Cole Hoyer-Winfield/ www.colehw.com*

CHAPTER ONE

Stencils

Opposite: Hardware stores, art suppliers, and craft outlets stock sets of letters and premade images for stenciling. Vintage sets sometimes turn up at flea markets and in secondhand stores.

Stenciling is the oldest known printing process. If you have ever heard of the prehistoric cave paintings in Altamira, Spain, or Lascaux, France, you might know that some of these 25,000-year-old images are actually stencils. Powdered charcoal was blown around the maker's hands to create beautiful images on the cave walls. I don't recommend spray-painting around your hand unless you have a rubber glove on, but there are many other natural and manmade objects recognizable by their silhouettes.

The cut-paper stencil is an ancient printing technique that has been raised to the level of an art form by many cultures. Today, it is experiencing a revival among graffiti artists and in obsessive installation art pieces.

SET NO. 29   3/4 INCH SHOW CARD ITALIC

ABCDE
I,M
R.

LETTER-IT YOURSELF

E·Z LETTER

STENCILS

SET NO. **89¢**
62

2½" **ROMAN**
Letters & Numbers
ACTUAL SIZE

**PROFESSIONAL
RESULTS EVERY TIME!**

E-Z LETTER is the
fast, economical
way for anyone to
letter easily and ac-
curately with per-

ABCDE

B
9

STENCIL YOUR OWN SIGNS WITH

A   1

B   *Studio Stencils*   2

C   3

ALPHABET and NUMERAL
Lettering
Stencils

JOHN DOE

IN SIZES
2½" - 3" - 4"

LOS ANGELES 35, CALIF.

R

THE BARE ESSENTIALS

- Felt markers
- Utility knife
- Masking tape or clear packing tape
- Paint, such as spray paint
- Ink (Speedball and Akua water-based block-printing inks are easy to clean up but don't react well to the outdoor elements or machine washing. Graphic Chemical, Gamblin, and Daniel Smith are some common brands of oil-based block-print inks that work well for stencils and are very permanent.)
- Solvent, such as kerosene, soybean oil, or corn oil in a pinch
- Soft rubber roller or brayer (Avoid hard rollers.)
- Paper
- Palette (This can be any flat nonporous surface, such as a piece of glass or an old tray or dinner plate.)
- Mechanic's soap for your hands
- Paper towels or rags for cleanup

You can use a Xerox or printout of a scanned image as your visual source material or make your own drawing. High-contrast images without many fine lines or technically complex cuts make the best stencils. They print more easily for you and read more easily for the viewer.

Making or Finding the Stencil

If you don't want to cut into your tabletop, be sure to lay cardboard under the stencil you are cutting. Using a mat knife, X-Acto, or razor blade, simply cut away the areas you wish to print—that is, the areas that will end up inked or painted. So, if you drew with a black marker, cut away the black areas. A nice advanced tool is a swivel knife, whose head revolves on tiny ball bearings and allows for smooth curvy cutting. (By the way, have you had your tetanus shots updated?)

Now, this presents a problem, as certain letters have floaty bits or areas that, once cut out, will no longer be attached to the body of the stencil paper—the two holes in the letter B, for example. Thankfully, you do not have to reinvent the wheel. Several computer fonts designed to be readable as cut images are readily available. These fonts have tabs or bridges that connect the holes in letters to the overall stencil background. This inherent limitation of stencil fonts can be used to graphic advantage as these font styles make for bold shapes that are quite readable, with lots of visual impact. (The military in many countries stencil their property in no-nonsense, clear-reading letters of this type.) Choose a large font size, 48-point or greater, not just for visual impact but because small typefaces are hard to cut well.

BAUHAUS 93

PORTAGO ITC

BRAGADOCCIO

HARVESTER

STENCIL

Many stencil-type fonts with tabs are readily available on computers, designed to be readable as cut images. The paper tabs link open spaces, such as the holes in letters, to the rest of the stencil.

Some of the oldest known manmade artworks are actually stencils. The makers blew powdered pigment around their hands in repeatable patterns. *Pablo H. Caridad/Shutterstock*

You might think a heavier paper or even thick cardboard would be a good choice for stencils, but actually a thin, though not too absorbent, paper (such as the stock used for manila folders) works quite well. One problem with thick paper is you lose detail both when you cut and when you print. Some people like to use Mylar plastic, but beginners should be cautioned that spray paint can leak under the plastic and mess up your print. Avoid overcuts at the corners of images and letters, as those little slices will leak.

Another stencil material option is frisket, a translucent and flexible plastic film that is adhesive on one side with a peel-off backing. It cuts easily with an X-Acto and can be bent over curved surfaces. It works well on bodies of automobiles, bicycles, drum kits, and guitars as well as on glass and Plexiglas windows. Plus, frisket tacks lightly and doesn't leave residue behind. A DIY version can be made with wide packing tape rolled out in sections on a smooth surface such as

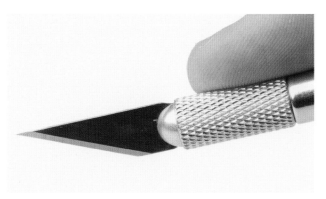

When cutting your own stencils, you can use an X-Acto or razor blade to cut away the areas you wish to print. Try to avoid overcuts—those little slices at the edges of stencil openings leak when painted. *Brent Hofacker/Shutterstock*

A swivel knife is another handy tool for cutting stencils. Its head revolves on tiny ball bearings, thus allowing for smooth curvy cutting. *Peter Morley/Shutterstock*

Simple hand-cut stencil for a Night Market booklet. The Night Market concept is an alternative barter/free-exchange economy in a festival setting. This particular event raised funds for the Solidago Ride, a women's bicycle tour around Lake Superior. *Solidago* is the genus of goldenrod, a flower indigenous to the Great Lakes region. *Artists: Rose Holdorf and Jacque Kutvirt*

TIP Once you gain a bit of experience, consider investing in Mylar plastic, frisket, or heavy brown paper for stencils, a swivel knife, and higher-quality paints with denser pigments. All can be found in art supply stores.

glass. With a transparent stencil material, the artist can place a design to be copied underneath and trace while cutting. In the case of clear tape, unroll some onto glass, place the item to be copied under the glass, and start slicing. Blades may get dull fast this way, but with a high-contrast image a careful tracer can achieve nearly photographic reproduction. *Note:* Tape used as a stencil might stick to and/or peel up underlying layers of paint or leave an unwanted sticky residue, so try out a piece in a discreet spot before committing to this

method. Adhesive material stencils don't work well on bumpy surfaces, such as brick or cement (the paint leaks underneath the stencil and the adhesive fails), or on fluffy, fibrous paper (the stencil gets permanently stuck to the paper).

Hardware stores and craft outlets often stock simple sets of cardboard letters or cutesy premade images for stenciling. Found objects that are flat and have definable edges, such as plastic toy letters, refrigerator magnets, bicycle parts, and more, can also serve as good ready-made stencils. Vinyl stick-on letters are another option, while some people use masking tape as a stencil material; it sticks well, resists paint, and comes in different widths. Paint stores offer premium masking tapes designed to stand up to drippy paint, so if this becomes a preferred method, consider investing in better tape products. Of course, your stencil will get inky or coated with paint, so whatever you use, choose something you're willing to sacrifice.

Making Oversize Stencils

Oversize stencils from smaller source images for use in murals or large posters can be made in one of three ways: using an opaque projector, page tiling, or with a digital projector. An opaque projector enlarges and displays original drawings and photos (unlike an overhead projector, which uses transparencies) by shining a bright light onto the object from above. Lenses and mirrors focus the enlarged image onto a viewing screen or wall where it can be traced and copied by hand onto big stencil paper. A range of models are available—from the inexpensive Porta-Trace, which only takes very small originals under 4 inches square; to the midrange Artograph with its 7x7-inch capacity and priced at about $180; to pricier models such as the Kopykake Kobra K5000, which for $600 will allow 8.5x11-inch source material. Large professional opaque projectors cost thousands of dollars. Sometimes these devices can be found secondhand.

A computer with Adobe Acrobat Pro or Acrobat Reader 10.1 or above will allow you to print large-length or -width PDF files using the tiling function. Print tiling refers to consecutive printouts of normal letter-size paper with the image cut into slightly overlapping sections. These multiple printouts can be taped together to make

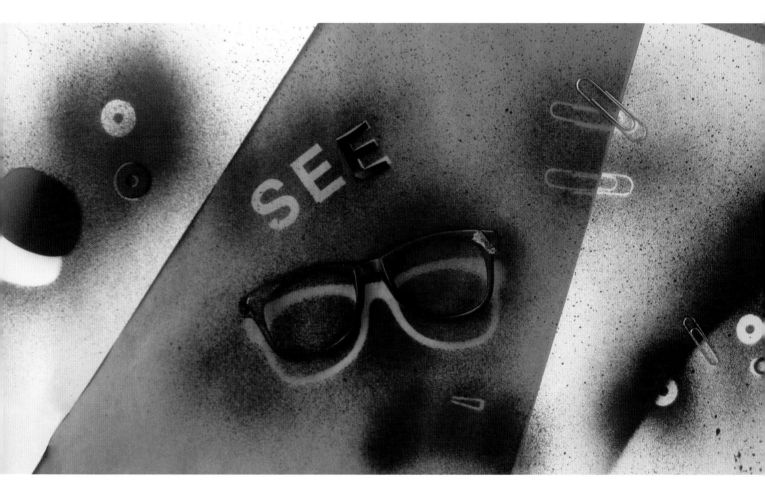

Found objects that are relatively flat and have good silhouettes can function as spray-around stencil items. So can stick-on vinyl letters, refrigerator magnets, toys, and cut-out pieces of cardboard. Just don't use anything that you don't want to get covered in paint.

a large stencil for cutting and printing. Save a Word or Photoshop document as a PDF, close it, and reopen it in Acrobat. Pull down the File menu and select Print. In the Print dialogue box, change Scale Image to Fit Page. Also deselect any box that says "Center Image." Instead select Page Scaling: Tile Large Pages. Tile Scale should be 100 percent plus an overlap of .005 or more. Now print. The image will come out in an ordered sequence of 8.5x11 sheets that can be reassembled into a large document. The overlap will facilitate taping the sheets together. Cut as needed. Illustrator files can also be tiled, but Acrobat Reader is commonly found on many computers and can be downloaded for free. Inexplicably, Photoshop currently doesn't seem to have the tiling option for printing.

If you have access to a computer and digital projector, they can be used together like an opaque projector. Scan the photo or drawing or create it in a graphics program. Programs such as Photoshop allow the designer to adjust contrast and detail, usefully mimicking a stencil. Try converting the image to black and white by choosing Grayscale, which can be found under Mode in the Image drop-down menu. Then use the Posterize effect under Adjustments, also in the Image drop-down list. You can also try the Filter, Sketch, or Photocopy effects on a grayscale image. Project the image file onto a wall where it can be traced by hand onto large stencil paper. Then cut as needed.

On the high end in terms of expense and equipment is the laser cutter. Digital files are sent to a computer-controlled laser that cuts paper or cardboard stencils to exact specifications. Some cooperative design shops and art schools offer access to such high-tech devices. Online services are also available. Vector files, such as those made in Illustrator, are required, so this machinery requires some graphics software experience. Laser-cut stencils are perfect and perfectly repeatable, so this method has clear advantages, even though it is very resource intensive. Perfect edges also look different than the distinctive softer edge of a homemade, hand-cut stencil, so consider the visual effect of each method.

Printing the Stencil

Once you have your stencils, prepare the surface you wish to print, while your hands are still clean. One advantage of stenciling is that almost any material can be stencil printed, from tissue-thin Japanese art paper, to T-shirts, to plastic CD covers, to bricks. The actual printing is accomplished by one of several methods.

Spray Paint

Shake the can for the full minute the manufacturer recommends. You want a fine mist, with well-distributed pigment. Caution: you must have a well-ventilated space when you use spray paint—it is quite bad for your liver and brain cells when breathed in an enclosed environment. Rubber gloves are not a bad idea, either.

Lay the stencil on top of the surface to be painted and spray in an even back-and-forth motion 8 to 12 inches away from the material. Get too close and the image will run; spray too far away and it will be too light or it may skip details. You will have to experiment to find out how many times the stencil can be used before it gets too soggy with paint. You might notice a tendency for the stencil's edges to curl up once they get wet with paint. You can make a few tiny rolls of masking tape in advance to stick under the edges if this becomes a problem. Let the image dry fully before lifting the stencil.

The solvents in aerosols are bad for your brain and liver. Be sure to use a respirator when using spray paint. And always paint in a well-ventilated area. *BortN66/Shutterstock*

Spray paint is available in a plethora of colors. The cheap store-brand stuff is perfectly fine for beginner stencil applications. You may wish to invest in higher-quality paints with finer pigment particles once your skills develop. *Franck Boston/Shutterstock*

Lay the stencil on top of your paper or material and move the spray can in an even back-and-forth motion 8 to 12 inches from the material. Try not to use a zigzag pattern. Spraying lightly in several coats helps preserve detail and prevents runs and drips.

Experiment to find out how many times your stencil can be printed before becoming soggy and unusable.

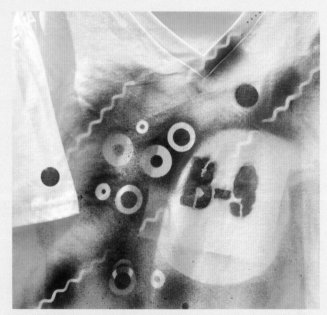

T-shirts are very absorbent, so don't use images that are too detailed when stenciling with spray paint. Both found-object stencils and cutout letters were used to create the design on this shirt.

Masking tape can be used to hold a paper stencil to a vertical surface, such as a wall, fence, or car door. Spraying on vertical surfaces takes some practice, as gravity comes into play. Paint drips downward and can leak under the top edges of stencils. Lighten up your coats and go over vertical surfaces in repeated horizontal passes of the spray can. Don't zigzag the spray paint path—go lightly back over the area in the same direction. Stop frequently to shake the can.

When stenciling multiple layers of color, let the first coat of paint dry before overcoating if possible. Sometimes different colors of wet spray interact in wonky ways to make alligator-skin textures. If that's not the effect desired, take a break between switching colors.

The Spray/Roll Method for Negative Silhouettes

Take a leaf, stick-on letter, masking tape, or other flat found object, lay it down on a piece of clean paper, and spray-paint or roll ink over it with a soft rubber roller. You'll get a decent image in negative clearly showing the object's outline and contours. Lift the object with tweezers or a toothpick soon after spraying or rolling.

Above and below: Roll around flat objects with interesting outlines or silhouettes to produce negative images.

Use a soft rubber roller or brayer to roll a slab of ink onto your palette. Leaving the roller on the slab while only moving it forward and backward won't coat the roller or spread the ink. Instead, repeatedly pick up the roller and scooch it forward. You should hear a nice *sch, sch* sound known as "sizzle" when the slab is properly rolled out. It'll look smooth, even, and velvety.

A leaf, paper cutout, or other object rolled with ink can be used as a stamp. Experiment with materials with prominent raised patterns. With some leaves' veins, for example, ink will print with near photographic detail. Pieces of cloth or textured paper, the bottom of old sneakers, and bike tires can all be inked and printed as stamps. Be sure to only use items that you don't mind getting inky.

In roll-up positive stamping, the printed image will be backward, so ink up the reverse, or wrong-reading, side.

You can repeat this image until the stencil object breaks down or gets too soggy with paint or ink. Experiment with objects that have an interesting outline or silhouette.

The Roll-Up Method, for Positive Images

Take a leaf, stick-on letter, or other flat found object, lay it down on a piece of Plexi or Mylar, or on an old dinner tray or a plastic plate, and roll ink over it with a soft rubber roller. Pick up the inked item, lay it ink side down on a piece of clean paper, and lay another piece of paper on top of the back of the inky item. Rub the top paper to offset the ink from the inked item onto the bottom piece of paper. When you lift the top sheet and the inky item, you will have an image of the item, in reverse, on the bottom paper. You are basically making a stamp out of your found object. Remember, the printed image will be backward with this method, so pay attention when inking letters so that you ink the "wrong" side.

Crayon and Chalk Rubbing Stencils

Paper stencils can also be printed with crayons and sticks of chalk or charcoal. Unwrap any paper and use the sides of these tools to rub over the stencil in broad, flat strokes. Rub across fine details carefully and in one direction. Hold the stencil firmly, have a friend hold it in place, or tape it down well over the paper to be printed, as stencil edges and tabs tend to fold and wrinkle under this method.

Crayons have an association with childhood, so they can work well for particular graphics invoking nostalgia and innocence. Charcoal on paper needs to be sprayed with a clear fixative spray afterward so it doesn't all rub off. Sidewalk chalk made for children is designed to wash away, so some guerilla chalking of upcoming events is a relatively harmless form of street graffiti, quickly remedied if confronted by authorities.

Stenciling on Paper and Stickers

When printing on paper with handmade stencils, examine the kind of paper you select. Some papers are so absorbent they are like bath towels—good for sopping up liquids, but resulting in letters and images with leaky or bleeding edges. Conversely, printing on plastic or coated stock (paper sealed with a chemical coating) that is too slick means your image may never dry. You won't be able to stack the prints up without them sticking to each other and probably getting paint all over you, too. Use paper that has a good balance between absorbency and printability. Brown craft paper, copier paper, and newsprint are inexpensive and work well. Bristol paper and Mohawk Superfine are higher-end examples of papers that take spray paint stenciling with good results. Since they are manufactured from paper pulp without acid, they have an added advantage of being considered archival and will last years without yellowing. Construction paper and paper towels, being fluffier, tend to bleed and blur, *plus* crumble with age because they're made with acidified materials.

Stenciling on T-Shirts and Other Fabric

New T-shirts usually have starch or silicon sprayed on them so they feel nice to shoppers. Wash new T-shirts before printing or these coatings will prevent the paint from completely sticking to the fabric. Also, T-shirts are naturally quite absorbent, so don't try to stencil images that are too fine or detailed when using spray paint.

Before stenciling, stuff the T-shirt with a piece of cardboard the same width as the shirt. This will make a nice flat, smooth surface for you to stencil on and keep the paint from leaking through to the back of the shirt. Don't overstretch the fabric of the shirt, though. When you paint on stretched fabric, the image looks warped when it snaps back to normal. If you have masking tape, you can tape the sleeves back behind the cardboard to keep them from flopping onto your stencil. Stuff all your shirts and do all your taping in advance while your hands are still clean.

Almost any store-brand spray paint will work well for T-shirt stenciling and the pigment will be fairly

TIP If you buy T-shirts new, save money by buying packs of three or five online or at a big-box store. Thrift stores usually stock tons of cheap T-shirts. Have some fun overprinting your graphics on top of preexisting commercial logos, mascots, etc. Wash any silicone or fabric softener out of the material before printing.

permanent. Spray lightly in a smooth back-and-forth motion, 8 to 10 inches from the shirt. Short bursts will keep the nozzle from clogging.

After the shirts are dry, ironing will help the image stay in the fabric. Put a piece of clean paper on the painted surface so your iron doesn't get gummed up with burnt paint. Warn your customers and band mates that the first few washings of those shirts should be done separately from other clothes. After that, wash as normal.

Other pieces of fabric, such as patches, can be printed via stenciling or other methods described later, and distributed to be pinned or sewn onto jackets, backpacks, or jeans. Material can be purchased at a fabric store by the yard or found secondhand. Select fabric that is relatively easy to print on. Make sure it isn't too rough (burlap, corduroy) or open-weave (netting, mesh), so that printed details won't be lost. Cotton and polyester sheets work great. Wash the cloth first and dry thoroughly, then iron it before printing. A smooth surface holds detail better. Patches are commonly about postcard size, 4x5 inches or so, but bandanas, flags, and banners are all doable. Leave some border around the design for sewing and pinning edges. Spray paint can really soak through cloth, so consider placing newsprint underneath to protect your work surface and spray lightly. Have fun finding unusual cloth patterns, kiddie-theme bedsheets, and the like to overprint with your own graphics.

Troubleshooting and Cleanup

Even experienced printers lose some products. Count on sacrificing a few T-shirts and posters to the learning curve. If your stencil is giving you trouble, stop after a couple of prints and be willing to modify your design for ease of printing.

Graffiti artists know well the problems that can develop with aerosol cans. Shaking the can well and stopping periodically to shake it again while painting will help. If the nozzle clogs, remove it and poke it with a pin. Caution: don't try poking the nozzle while it is attached to the can—you can get an eyeful of painful spray paint and solvent. Sometimes holding the can upside down for a brief burst of spray will clear a clogged nozzle.

If you used a roller or brayer, after printing, roll it out on cheap paper or old newspapers until most of the ink is off. This will minimize the amount of solvent needed for final cleanup. If water-based ink was used, run the brayer under warm water until the ink is gone. Be sure to dry it thoroughly so the metal parts don't rust. If you used oil-based ink, in a ventilated area or outdoors, and wearing rubber gloves, pour a small amount of a solvent, such as kerosene, over the roller and roll it on more newspapers. Soybean oil solvents are becoming more commonly available and work well to dissolve oil-based ink. Even corn oil can be used in place of solvents; just check whether coworkers have allergies to these substances. Do a final wipe with a paper towel. Don't forget to wipe behind the brayer's "ears" (the sides of the cylinder). If you are using a professional shop, ask what solvent it prefers for its tools. The composite plastic or gelatin in some expensive brayers breaks down under vegetable oil.

A single-edge razor blade can get almost every bit of ink off a glass palette, and vigorous wiping with a paper towel can remove the rest. Minimize your use of and exposure to solvents when possible.

Rubber gloves are handy, but mechanic's soap (such as Gojo or Goop) is very effective at cleaning spray paint and ink off your hands. Soap up dry hands, rub to dissolve the paint, and wipe your hands dry with a paper towel or rag. Only use water and soap after that initial "dry" round. Much more paint will come off that way. A short scrub with a soft brush is another good idea. Some people prefer pumice bar soap, such as Boraxo. Mechanic's soap can also contain pumice, which helps scrub hands clean. Don't eat finger food or smoke until after all ink is off.

Gojo can also be used on a rag to remove paint from surfaces where it isn't wanted. Don't use it on someone's good furniture, though, as it can remove varnish.

STENCIL IDEAS

Two details of a mural by Broken Crow, a stencil-based collaboration between Mike Fitzsimmons and John Grider. The two liken the process to making a giant coloring book outline on the wall, filling it in with color, and then restenciling the wall with their signature detailed textures. The stencils require months of drawing preparation and are cut by hand in manageable sections of heavy paper. This piece shows how a stencil can be printed in any color, making a repeated image pleasingly variable. Broken Crow murals can be found in Minneapolis, St. Paul, Duluth, Milwaukee, Chicago, Baltimore, Reno, Nashville, Austin, Dallas, Mexico, New York, Paris, London, and Africa. www.brokencrow.com

STENCIL IDEAS

SLEDGE OF RESISTANCE

PRISONS
TWO MILLION AMERICANS IN CAGES
DON'T WORK

Josh MacPhee, author of the book *Stencil Pirates*, made this stencil as part of the Cut and Paint project (www.cutandpaint.org) featuring downloadable graphics for DIY stenciling.

The Sledge of Resistance hammers at the machines of repression in this dynamic stencil poster in the Russian Constructivist style. It was used for the invitation to an exhibit called "The Beauty of Subversity," a national exhibition of alternative poster art held at Speedboat Gallery in St. Paul, Minnesota, which hosted punk rock shows in the basement. *Courtesy Kevin Adress*

My car, entirely hand stenciled with found objects in a process I call "Godolleization." Here I used gears, gaskets, computer parts, and multiple layers of automotive paint and Rust-Oleum. I've also stenciled a racing motorcycle, furniture, a violin, and a drum kit in this postindustrial style.

In his piece *The Man Who Waits for the Mermaids*, Steve Griffin hand stenciled bed sheets using masking tape and spray paint, then outlined with a marker.

The 1992 Farmers Union Grain Terminal Association grain elevator mural by Sara Rotholz Weiner in south Minneapolis used "stencils" created by the shadows from the nearby high-tension towers.

During a light-rail construction project, the Irrigate Project in St. Paul, Minnesota, hired Broken Crow to design a downloadable 11x17-inch stencil on the theme of Art Happens Here. Handy instructions include the following: "Make sure you have permission to spray the image on a surface besides your own!" *www.irrigatearts.org*

THE HOLD STEADY

Brooklyn, New York, band The Hold Steady employed these simple die-cut cardboard stencils to mark their road cases. Though the stencils have reached the end of their intended use, they now make for a striking visual. *Courtesy Tad Kubler*

Crude but effective, the hand-cut and hand-stenciled eponymous 7-inch record by Austin, Texas, band Cruddy represents the epitome of work ethic. A limited edition of 300 copies means carefully spray-painting 300 times. The sleeve was designed by Cruddy guitarist/vocalist Drew Schmitz; the record was released by Let's Pretend Records in Bloomington, Indiana. *www.cruddymusicforcruddypeople.com*

2

Linocuts
and Woodcuts

In printing, "relief" refers to a raised surface that is inked and printed. Relief printing with carved wood blocks is a very old and nearly worldwide process developed to a high art in ancient China and Japan, medieval Europe, India, the Pacific islands, Africa, and Latin America. Solid soft woods like basswood work well for relief printing but can be difficult to find in large chunks. Today, linoleum is a cheap, readily available, and more easily carved alternative to wood. Made from ground wood chips and resin, linoleum is available mounted on blocks and baked into sheets with a backing material, such as burlap. It is usually gray or brick red.

Getting into linocut relief printing can be fairly inexpensive. The main tools you'll need are (from left) a baren for applying pressure when offsetting the ink to paper, a soft rubber roller, or a brayer for applying ink to the linoleum, and a gouging tool handle with an assortment of interchangeable blades for carving the linoleum. *MCarper/Shutterstock*

THE BARE ESSENTIALS

- Linoleum (or wood blocks)
- Carving tools
- Ink (Akua is a good brand of water-based block-printing ink. Graphic Chemical, Gamblin, and Daniel Smith are some common brands of oil-based block print inks that work well for relief prints and are very permanent.)
- Solvent, such as kerosene, mineral spirits, soy bean oil, or corn oil in a pinch
- Spatula
- Roller or brayer
- Palette (This can be any flat nonporous surface, such as a piece of glass or an old tray or dinner plate.)
- Wooden spoon or baren
- Paper
- Mechanic's soap
- Rubber gloves (if using oil-based ink)
- Rags or paper towels

Optional: printing press, movable type, fancy paper, a single-edge razor blade for cleanup. Purchase your linoleum, ink, and tools at an art supply or craft store.

Drawing

Relief prints made with linoleum are often referred to as linocuts. The first step to creating a linocut is to draw your image and/or lettering on the linoleum to be carved. Many people like to use black felt markers for this step because the wide marks mimic the effect of printing ink. Remember, the image on the block needs to be backward in relation to the printed image, so be sure to draw words, numbers, maps, etc. backward on the linoleum.

In addition, keep in mind that the top surfaces (i.e., those you *don't* carve) will receive ink, while anything carved away will *not*. One way to think about this is to imagine you will be inking the tops of the mesas in a landscape while all the canyons will stay free of ink. The inky roller will skip over anything you have carved out, so in a black-and-white print, the carved lines are white. So if you use a black marker, when it comes time to carve leave the black areas alone and scoop out everything else.

Preexisting images can be transferred to a linoleum or wood block in one of two ways: by tracing or using solvent to release photocopy toner onto the block. Trace through an image from behind with carbon paper using the firm pressure of a pencil or pen. You can make your own "carbon" paper by blackening an intermediary clean sheet of paper with a stick of charcoal. Lay the charcoal-covered sheet face down on the linoleum block, place the image you wish to trace face down over the intermediate sheet, and trace firmly. The carbon will offset onto the block, leaving black areas that can be carved around. Images are traced from behind so they are reproduced backward on the block, which, as previously mentioned, is necessary for the inked image to print forward. Use a thin paper with a strong enough image so it can be seen through the back for tracing.

TIP

Draw your images or write your words forward (the right way) on thin paper, then flip the paper over and tape it to a window so you have a reference of how it should look when you draw it on your linoleum or wood block.

This can also be a useful technique for carbon paper transfers. Outline an image taped to a window on the back of the paper as it's illuminated through the glass. This will give you a properly backward image. Then retrace it with a piece of carbon paper onto a printing block.

Carving

Next, it's time to carve your design. Speedball makes very affordable and reliable linoleum carving gouges. Buy a handle and some interchangeable blades online or at an art supply store. I don't recommend the prepackaged gouge sets, but instead buy some V-shaped gouges and some U-shaped gouges in both small and large widths. A sturdy utility knife may come in handy for scoring and cutting, too. Slightly more pricey, but worth the money, are sets of balsawood-handled Japanese carving tools.

Remember to always carve away from you and keep vital veins (like those in your wrists) out of the path of sharp tools, which can slip while you carve.

Strong solvents, such as acetone (nail polish remover), lighter fluid, mineral spirits, and wintergreen oil, can all be used to induce the toner on a photocopied image to release onto another surface. Only do this in a well-ventilated space or outdoors, and wear rubber gloves. A fresh photocopy works best, as some laser and inkjet prints make the toner cling too well, so experiment with various machines. Place the photocopy face down onto the printing block, taping it in place. Using a cotton swab or paper towel, distribute a small amount of solvent onto black areas on the back of the photocopy. Don't pour a huge pool of it, just moisten the paper and then rub the image with a wooden spoon. The image will start to show through the back of the wet paper. Rub firmly to release all the detail. Continue working across the image, applying solvent and rubbing until the entire image is transferred onto the printing block. Peel up the copy paper. When dry, the image can be carved like any drawing.

Speedball makes very affordable linoleum carving gouges. I prefer to have some V-shaped gouges and some U-shaped gouges in both small and large widths. *Courtesy Speedball Art Products®*

Carving linoleum with gouges is inexpensive and relatively easy once you warm it up. The resin melts slightly and makes the linoleum more pliable. *Demonstrated by Erin Holt*

Once you have a nice slab of ink, start rolling onto the linoleum and then return often to the slab to pick up more ink. Remember to keep scooching the roller forward on the slab for an even coating of ink.

Lay printing paper down gently and don't move it once it's down. Start in the middle and gently spread the paper out toward the sides.

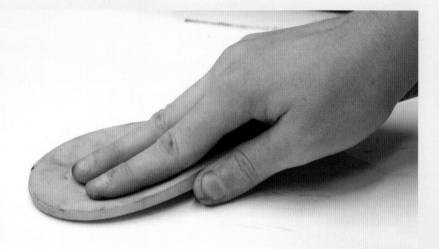

Rub the back of the paper firmly in small circular motions. You'll know you're rubbing hard enough when your hands become warm from the friction. You will start to see the image appear through the back of the paper.

Test prints are called proofs. The term "proofreading" comes from this checking of the first test prints for typos and other errors. This is your chance to see if everything looks good enough to keep printing.

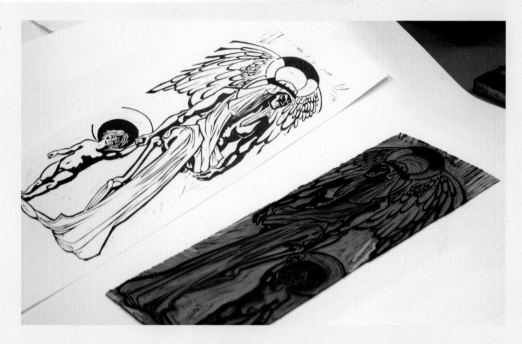

I recommend sheets of burlap-backed linoleum rather than linoleum mounted on wood blocks. They are cheaper and easier to warm up. A heat source will make your linoleum soft and much more easy to carve. Remember, linoleum is made of ground wood chips and resin, so trying to carve it cold will result in a lot of cracks and require more effort on your part. Warming it will allow you to carve fluid curvy lines into the linoleum as if it were butter. Always use a passive or indirect method of heating linoleum. One way to warm a piece of linoleum is to cover it with paper and use a clothes iron. You might also heat a flat-bottom frying pan on the stove and set it on top of the paper-covered linoleum. Using an oven to heat linoleum is a very bad idea, as is putting the iron or other heat source directly on it, because the hot resin becomes stinky. Putting the linoleum over a direct flame may catch the burlap backing on fire. And a microwave is definitely *not* a good heat source to warm linoleum, as it may cause it to explode.

You need to carve down only about $1/8$ inch. There is no need to dig to the bottom of the linoleum. Again, as you carve the material, remember that the uncut stuff, the relief surface, is what will be inked and printed. Anything you carve away won't print.

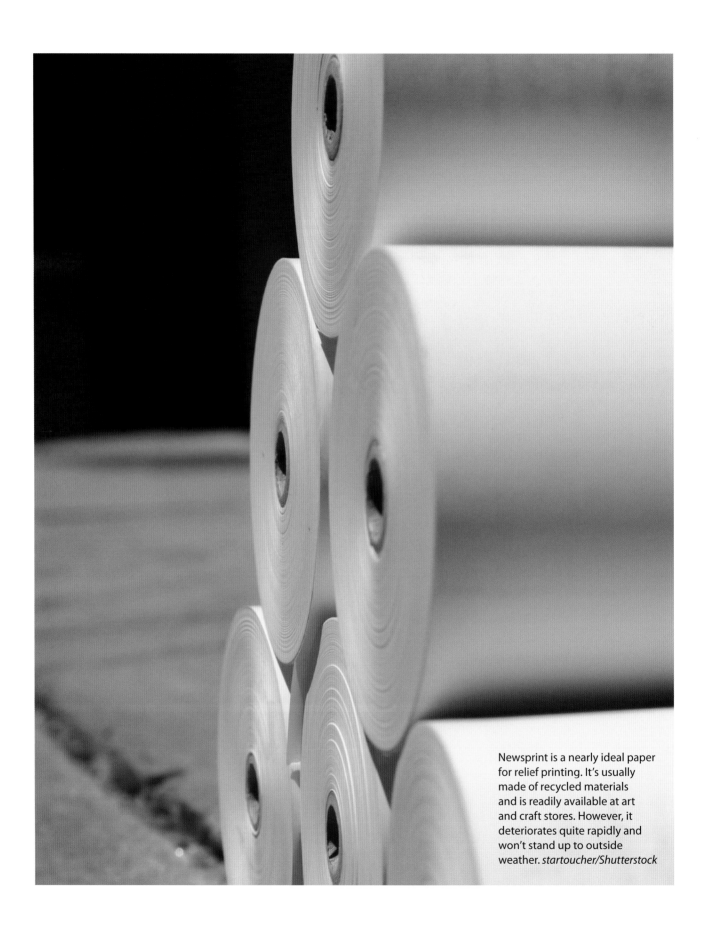

Newsprint is a nearly ideal paper for relief printing. It's usually made of recycled materials and is readily available at art and craft stores. However, it deteriorates quite rapidly and won't stand up to outside weather. *startoucher/Shutterstock*

Above and below: Block-printing ink is available in both water- and oil-based forms. Each has its advantages and disadvantages in regard to ease of cleanup and durability. *Courtesy Speedball Art Products®*

Paper

Paper used for relief printing needs to be smooth and fairly lightweight, especially if you're printing by hand. Consider using cheap paper for most of a run while including a few prints on higher-quality paper for posterity or for special situations. Newsprint is a nearly ideal cheap paper to print on. It's usually made of recycled materials and is readily available at art and craft stores. However, newsprint pulp is made with acid, so newsprint deteriorates quite rapidly and won't stand up to outside weather. Likewise, white and color copier paper is also acidified, although less so, so it eventually yellows and crumbles but not as quickly as newsprint. High-quality art papers, such as Japanese mulberry paper, come in a wider variety of colors and won't yellow and crumble over time. Another option is sticker paper, available at office supply stores. This typically comes in sheets with removable backing and is available in various colors. Stickers can be minimally weatherproofed by spraying the thoroughly dry prints with a clear coat spray paint or old-fashioned hairspray. Try it first on a scrap piece to make sure the spray overcoat doesn't react badly with the paper or ink.

Purchase or cut your paper several inches larger than your block all the way around. The margins will make it easy to lay it down and pick it up without messing up the actual image, especially if your fingers get inky. You can

cut it down to correct size when you're all done. Cut all the paper you will need in advance while your hands are still clean, and cut several extra pieces of inexpensive paper for your initial proofs (test prints) and for cleaning up when you are done. Assemble your stack of proofing and printing paper in a clean location near your printing area.

Inking

Ink usually comes in cans or tubes from an art supply store. You can use water-based block-printing ink from a manufacturer, such as Akua or Speedball. The advantage of these products is cleanup with soap and water. The disadvantages are that some water-based inks run if exposed to water (think rain) and tend to fade

Here's a letterpress poster I created using wooden type and a metal picture block of a motorcycle. The pointing hand is an example of a printer's ornament called a dingbat. The term has since come to imply a slightly loopy person, possibly derived from the decorative and unserious tone of these kinds of marks. Today, of course, fonts entirely containing dingbats are available for computers.

in strong sunlight. Oil-based inks, such as those from Speedball, Graphic Chemical, Gamblin, Daniel Smith, and Charbonnel, are more permanent, nonfading, and waterproof; however, they do require a solvent for cleanup and a well-ventilated space. Chemical-resistant rubber gloves like those used for stripping paint are also recommended during cleanup of oil-based inks.

Use a soft rubber roller or brayer appropriate to the size of the linoleum you have carved. In other words, a 1-inch-wide brayer, while fine for a 5-inch piece, will make it very hard to ink up a 5-foot-long piece of linoleum. You will also need a palette to roll out a slab of ink. This simply can be a clean and flat nonporous surface, such as a piece of glass, a dining hall tray, or a large dinner plate.

Begin by using your spatula to lay out a small bead of ink on the palette to the width of the roller. The palette can be a piece of window glass or Plexiglas, a dinner tray, or a large flat plate from a secondhand store. A plastic picnic plate can make a decent disposable palette in a pinch. Roll the bead into a smooth, even slab by continuously picking up the roller and scooching it forward and back in a straight line. Controlling your slab means the ink will be smoothly deposited on your linoleum and not glob up or be too thin when it prints. Once you have a nice slab, roll onto the linoleum two or three times until most of the ink is off the roller and on the block, then return to the slab to pick up more ink. Continue rolling and inking until the linoleum is full with a nice juicy coating of ink.

Pulling a Proof

To print, you may want to clean your hands first, then pick up a clean piece of proofing paper and waft it gently down over the inked linoleum. Once the paper has touched the ink surface, you will not be able to move it without blurring the image. Using a wooden spoon or a baren (a Japanese palm leaf rubbing tool), rub the back of the paper firmly in small circular motions, periodically lifting up a corner to check your progress. The circular rubbing will transfer the ink from the linoleum to the paper. Be sure to cover every area of the linoleum and try to keep your pressure even. You will see the image start to come through the back of the paper. That is a sign you are rubbing hard enough. Gently peel up the paper and, voila, you have a beautiful test print. No need to clean up just yet. You can continue inking, rolling, and pulling more proofs until you get the desired result. Clip the proofs back to back on a clothesline (another good reason for those wide margins), or lay them flat until they are dry. Oil-based ink can take several hours to dry, while water-based ink might be dry in half an hour.

Opposite: Woodcut poster for the Bring Out Yer Dead 2012 vintage motorcycle rally in Duluth, Minnesota. The Rolling Concours caption is a bit of humor, referring to high-tone vehicle-collector events. Black and white gives a great rough-and-ready feel; the angles impart speed and attitude. *Artist: Richard Cooter*

Used wood and metal letterpress type and image blocks can be found in antique stores. Individual blocks can be inked up and printed with a baren or a wooden spoon, but a revival of interest in this type of printing has meant more access to facilities with actual letterpresses. Some of these wooden typefaces date to the nineteenth century. The very slim, tall A is an example of Clarendon Double Extra Condensed. *Author collection*

Inking lines of metal type and an image with a hand brayer. The letters and images are locked into a Vandercook letterpress with metal shims called leading and wood spacers known as "furniture." Letterpress type and images are set backward so they will print forward. This inking process uses a much leaner slab and less ink than hand-rubbed linocuts or woodblock prints.

Your block may need more ink or more pressure. If the print looks speckled or salty or just too light, both are probably the case. Occasionally you may over-ink the block, resulting in fine details filling in with ink. This is easily solved by using a slightly leaner slab (i.e., scraping up some of the ink and rolling out the slab again).

Cleanup

I recommend stripping the ink off the linoleum by pulling prints onto clean paper sheets until almost no ink is left on the block. Next, use some of those too light prints to roll excess ink off your brayer until almost none is left. If you are thrifty, you can always use the backs of these sheets once the ink is dry for making test proofs of your next print. Ink on paper is fully recyclable, so there's no need to put them in the trash.

Scrape your palette free of excess ink with a razor blade or the spatula. If you used water-based ink, rinse off your linoleum and roller with warm water. If you used oil-based ink, put on gloves, open a window or go outside, and use a solvent on paper towels or a rag. Clean the ink off the linoleum, palette, spatula, and roller. Dispose of solvent-soaked rags properly; most shops use a metal can or a bucket with a tight-fitting lid so fumes don't build up in the work area. Use of a good mechanic's soap, such as Gojo, is always helpful in the final cleaning of your hands.

Repairs

Let's say you pull your first proof and one letter or a whole word is backward. Not a problem—use a utility knife to

Letterpress-printed poster advertising a meeting of eccentric vehicles. Here I used my large collection of antique printer's picture blocks and type. Some of these old metal illustrations were etched and mounted on wood; others were cast as whole metal blocks. It pays to keep your eyes open. A friend working as an elevator operator in a warehouse paid a trash remover $25 for a pallet full of wood and metal blocks like these and passed them on to me.

carve out that section. You can make a plug out of a small piece of new linoleum. Carve it correctly, place it in the hole you made, jigsaw style, and print again. How do you get the correct image to fit? Ink up and stamp the new piece of lino with the bad piece you carved out. Next, carve the new piece using the stamped area as a guide and it will fit perfectly. In fact, the jigsaw puzzle

Photopolymers, special plastics that react to light, can be used to make digital image files into plastic relief plates. These plastic plates are mounted onto wood blocks to make them printable in the letterpress. Note the block is mounted the same height as the wood type. Service bureaus, such as Smart Set (www.smartset.com), will custom make photopolymer plates for you from an uploaded file.

Independent Project Press (www.independentprojectpress.com) specializes in creating distinctive letterpress-printed objects, such as Discfolio all-cardboard CD packaging. The printed cardboard is scored, folded, and die cut. Think of die cutting as a cookie cutter for paper. Die-cutting services are found at specialty print shops, while craft stores sell simple home-use machines. It certainly beats hand cutting multiple items with scissors.

technique is another way to get multiple colors out of one lino block. If you have access to a power jigsaw, your block can be easily carved into multiple pieces, inked each in separate colors, reassembled, and printed as one unit—a nice effect.

Letterpress

Letterpress is a form of relief printing using wood, metal, and sometimes plastic-type and image blocks with a printing press. Like so many printing processes, letterpress was once the height of technology, used to print books, news, invitations, menus, and calling cards. Ben Franklin used this type of printing, as did Posada in

nineteenth-century Mexico. As other processes gained favor, the tools and equipment fell into artists' hands and the unique form stayed alive. Used wood and metal letterpress type and image blocks can be found in antique stores and online. Individual blocks can be inked up and printed with a baren or wooden spoon without a printing press, but a revival of interest in the process has meant more access to relief presses designed to print these blocks. Affordable small printing presses, such as tabletop clamshell presses with names like Kelsey and Excelsior, show up in online auctions and at yard sales. I strongly recommend getting some instruction in this process. Centers for book arts exist in major cities and offer classes and access programs. Art schools and

These 7-inch vinyl record covers from Independent Project Press use antique handset type and ornaments alongside digitally produced photopolymer plates to create specialty print designs for indie bands and record companies.

This handshake declares, "Love one another, help one another," an appropriate sentiment for the featured quote by Ben Sira, circa 180 BC. This two-color letterpress relief print is from a series of quotation postcards by Lunalux Studio. *www.lunalux.com*

cooperative studios may also house letterpress facilities. Hamilton Wood Type & Printing Museum in Two Rivers, Wisconsin, runs a museum devoted to the medium and holds classes.

Think of letterpress letters as sawn-up woodcut blocks. But long ago some smart person got everyone to agree to make the blocks all the same height so they'd be interchangeable, all fitting "type high" into a letterpress. The letters and woodcut, metal-cut, or linoleum images,

A faithful friend is a sturdy shelter; he that has found one has found a treasure. There is nothing so precious as a faithful friend & no scales can measure his excellence. — *Ben Sira*

This assortment of letterpress-printed items from Independent Project Press includes an Earth Day concert pass with a hole punched for a lanyard, a business card, and a gummed-back shipping sticker. The juxtaposition of recycled brown cardboard with bright colors and metallic inks creates a unique contrast.

type high and printed on a letterpress. Some presses have fancy features, such as grippers for holding the paper while it prints and automatic inkers (instead of rolling up by hand with a brayer). Some are even motorized. The results are beautiful and unique, as, unlike photocopies, letterpress prints have a distinctive dent or bite into the paper from the pressure of the press. Another advantage of a letterpress is that it enables high-volume output in a relatively short time, so if you have a lot of relief prints to make, you may explore learning how to operate such a press. Cleanup follows the earlier directions.

Relief Printing on T-Shirts

Linoleum and wood blocks print well on T-shirts with oil-based ink, provided the detail isn't too fine. Cloth tends to fill in fine lines or smudge them together.

It can be tricky to print a relief block by hand on a T-shirt. Stuff the shirt with smooth or corrugated cardboard covered with smooth paper (so the ridges don't interfere with printing). Ink up the block generously, lay it face down on the T-shirt, and lean heavily on all areas of the back of the block. Use all your weight so you apply enough pressure to offset the ink onto the shirt. Peel up the block and let the shirt dry overnight. After it is dry, you can help set the ink permanently by ironing the shirt from the back. Launder it separately the first few times.

also mounted on blocks made type high, are locked into the press bed with wooden blocks called furniture and thin metal shims called leading, holding them so there's no wiggle room. Magnets can also be used to snugly fit type blocks in place in the press. The type "face" or printable surface of the block is inked up and paper is placed over it just as in the other relief printing processes. Instead of a baren or spoon, a heavy top cylinder on the press is rolled over the inked blocks and paper, offsetting the ink onto the paper. Type and images are set backward so that they print forward.

Special plastics that react to light, called photopolymers, can be used to transform digital files into plastic relief plates so the imagery is no longer confined to hand-carved blocks. These plastic plates are mounted onto wood blocks to make them type high and printable in a letterpress. Similarly, linoleum can be mounted on a block

TIP

When printing on T-shirts, design your relief-printing block with big bold shapes and letters. Fine details tend to fill in when printed on cloth. When printing on patches, select fabric that isn't too textured—burlap and corduroy won't hold detail.

Here, artist JAO printed, flipped, and reprinted a wood block on a T-shirt. She uses scrap wood and expressionistic gestures to give her images dynamic flair. *www.jaoart.com*

Sean StarWars of Laurel, Mississippi, is an obsessive woodcut artist. He prints on T-shirts, bags, and glitter stickers, and even overprints posters on bits of preprinted billboard paper—this in addition to creating fine-art prints. This hand-printed Cajun gator has a squeezebox. Sean says gators love music. *www.seanstarwars.com*

Using a Car as Makeshift Printing Press

Applying pressure to all areas of the block is the key to success when relief printing on a T-shirt. If you don't have access to a press, a car can be used to aid in this step. After stuffing the shirt with cardboard and generously inking up your wood or linoleum block, lay it face down on the T-shirt in a dry, smooth driveway or parking lot. It helps if you lay the shirt on a piece of plywood, Masonite, fiberboard, or other large, smooth, and clean surface. Next, place mat board over the back of the linoleum to avoid getting tire tracks on your T-shirt. Now drive a car slowly over the block, mat-board backing and shirt. The pressure from the weight of the car will offset the ink to the fabric. Don't go too fast or you may shoot the block halfway down the street (more likely, your block will move and smudge the design). If your block is wider than a tire, turn the wheels slightly and run over the stack again slightly to one side, as needed. You may end up with some residual tire tracks, but they'll add character to your printed shirts.

Your car can function as makeshift printing press. Stuff a shirt with cardboard and lay it on the ground atop a smooth piece of plywood, Masonite, or fiberboard. Then ink up a linoleum block and place it face down on the shirt. Have a set of shirts stuffed with cardboard in advance to save time. *Demonstrated by Christian Behrends*

Place mat board (not foamboard or the brown corrugated stuff—they're too squishy) or a piece of light plywood or Masonite atop the linoleum.

Now slowly back over the stack. The pressure from the weight of the car will offset the ink to the material to be printed. Go slowly so the material doesn't shoot out from under the tire. If the linoleum is wider than the tire, turn the wheel slightly and roll back over the stack as needed. Inhabitants of northern climates know this "rocking" technique well from getting cars unstuck in the snow. As you can see, the top mat board keeps the tire tracks off your T-shirt. If you prefer that look, you can always omit the mat board.

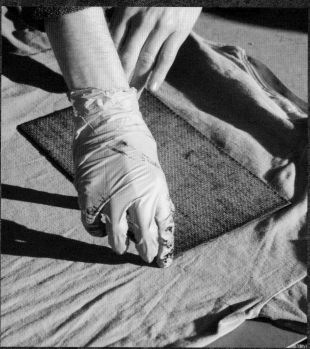

Gently peel up the linoleum. Don't shift it around too much or the detail will get smudged. *Demonstrated by Christian Behrends*

The finished print is a skyline image created by Arella Vargas. We're ready to re-ink the linoleum and do it again on the next shirt. Try to find a clean, smooth spot of pavement, not one full of gravel and potholes.

The Big Thing linoleum relief print. This event was an interactive multimedia extravaganza involving Indian dance, stilt walkers, music, and giant constructed costumes. *Artists: Gretchen Keiling and Lela Pierce*

RELIEF PRINTING IDEAS

Woodcut wheat pasted onto brick wall outside Bruno David Gallery, St. Louis, Missouri, presumably by street artist Swoon. Swoon skyrocketed to art-world fame with beautiful, intricate graphics applied to derelict urban spaces. She chose wheatpasting over direct graffiti so the work could be removed with water if there was an objection from building owners or tenants. Lately, few people object.

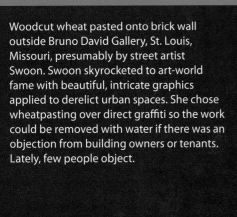

Head, linoleum relief–printed stickers. Nice use of a white line direct-carving technique.
Artist: Jeff Gillam

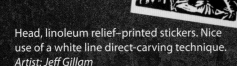

Vintage linoleum relief–printed stickers by Bikini Kill, an original riot grrrl band active in the 1990s. The irregular scissor-cut shapes add to the sentiment.

The true DIY collaborative spirit is evident in this vinyl 45-rpm record with hand-printed cover. Draghounds drummer Brien Lilja gouged and relief printed the original linoleum block. Next, using a photocopier, that design was made into two transparencies that were exposed for a photo screenprint. Brien and bandmate Darin Rinne screenprinted the covers, first in black then in red ink, with my help. Each sleeve was folded and glued by hand.

Bobby Birdman's 7-inch, "Don't Walk Away," on the Dub Narcotic label is part of a K Records series using a vintage stencil cutter found at a Boeing surplus warehouse. Calvin Johnson, founder of K, as well as this sleeve's designer, explained that the stencil cutter, letterpress printing, and a rubber stamp were used on pre-glued white paper sleeves. www.krecs.com

Spread the Ink, Spread the Love, detail of a relief-printed T-shirt. Drive By Press does live on-the-spot printing at rock shows, schools, and art events, bringing a mobile press as part of the road show. *Artists: Drive By Press/www.DrivebyPress.com*

47

Relief-print poster advocating for a minor league stadium uses a blend roll, shifting the color across the image from dark orange to light and matching the throwing action of the pitcher. Antique letterpress wooden type amplifies the nostalgic feel. *Artist: Bill Moran/ www.blincpublishing.com*

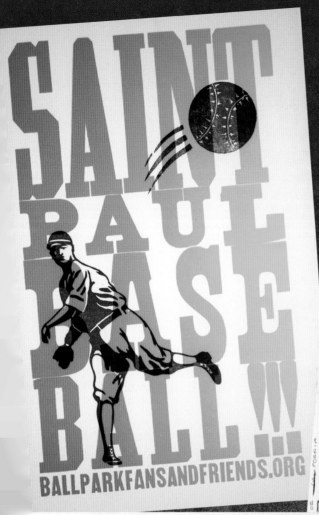

Product of California, a three-color woodblock relief print by Imin S. Yeh. Note the space made for the wheat stalk in the two orange blocks. This technique, called trapping, generates visual impact as the overlap pokes into the bending worker's space and draws the eye directly there. The "reduction" technique is also used. The artist carved the California shape, printed it 55 times, and then carved the design into that shape to overprint in dark orange. This is also known as a suicide print because the first block is sacrificed. *www.iminyeh.info*

La Lotería VI, a beautiful black-and-white relief print by Mexican artist Artemio Rodríguez. When Rodríguez updated the images from the iconic Mexican board game Lotería, he included social commentary and witty observations on human nature. *www.lamanografica.com*

Combining the vertical shape of the paper with a diagonal composition and breaking out of the frame creates a dynamic design in this hand-printed woodcut from the Firecracker Press. *www.firecrackerpress.com*

Colleen Stockmann used assorted mismatched type and ornaments to create a lovely letterpress-printed calendar. Each month has a different typographic composition in a different color. July is set in subtle red and gray on the warm white Canal paper by St-Armand. Stockmann founded Analogue Anatomy Press (www.analogueanatomy.blogspot.com).

A Ralph Waldo Emerson quote printed with letterpress on dark blue paper with silver ink. Lunalux Studio (www.lunalux.com) designs and prints invitations, stationery, calling cards, announcements, and posters using vintage printing presses.

A singer and a musician from Hokusai Manga Vol. 11 (1834). Katsushika Hokusai invented the form of Manga ("scenes from everyday life"), authoring detailed woodcut-print books that were incredibly popular in nineteenth-century Japan. These books featured amazing characters, including demons, monsters, musicians, artists, workers, and nobles printed in three colors: black, gray, and peach. They are the inspiration for the comic book and anime forms today. *Author collection*

WRITE IT*ON*YOUR heart THAT*EVERY DAY•IS•THE BEST DAY*OF THE year

···I RALPH WALDO EMERSON I···

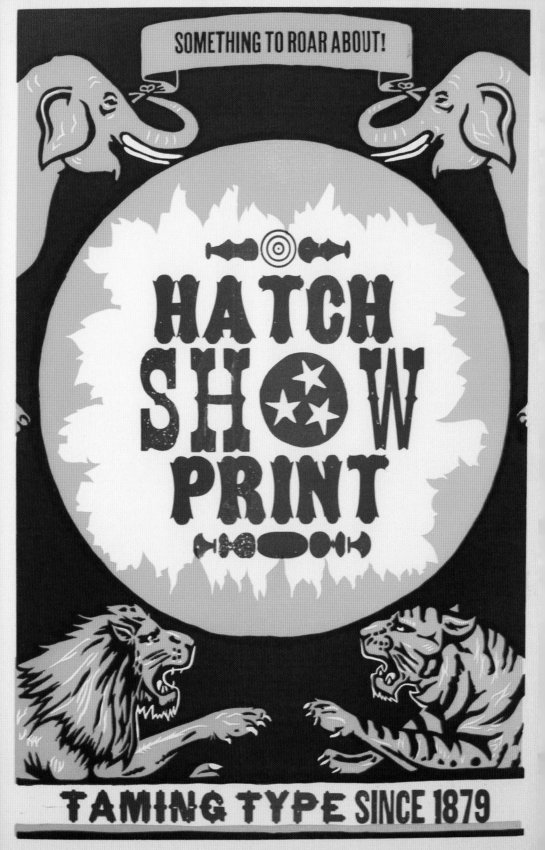

Hatch Show Print was founded in 1879 to print posters advertising circuses, sporting events, vaudeville acts, and operas. Eventually they began doing gig posters for the Grand Ole Opry. Hatch Print also produced tour posters for a stunning array of music legends, from Bill Monroe and Hank Williams to Patsy Cline and Johnny Cash. *Courtesy Hatch Show Print/www.hatchshowprint.com*

One of the oldest working letterpress print shops in America, Hatch Show Print is also a museum, store, and historical archive overseen by manager, curator, and chief designer Jim Sherraden. You can see tens of thousands of antique wood blocks and printing plates, as well as vintage presses, in operation at Hatch. It is open to the public with a beautiful array of hand-printed items on offer. *Courtesy Hatch Show Print/ www.hatchshowprint.com*

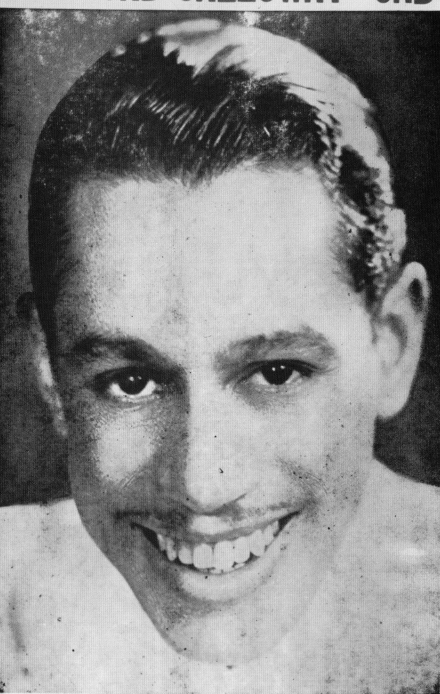

CAB CALLOWAY CAB CALLOWAY CAB CALLOWAY LLOWAY CAB CALLOWAY CAB CALLOWAY CAB CALLOWAY CAB CALLOWAY CAB CALLOWAY CAB CALLOWAY

Hatch Show Print is now part of the Country Music Hall of Fame and Museum and a tourist destination in Nashville, Tennessee. It still prints and sells fabulous posters commemorating past acts, such as Louis Armstrong and Cab Calloway, from antique type and picture plates. Hatch also prints for contemporary big-ticket artists such as The White Stripes, Bon Iver, and Wilco with the distinctive look of letterpress relief prints. *Courtesy Hatch Show Print/www.hatchshowprint.com*

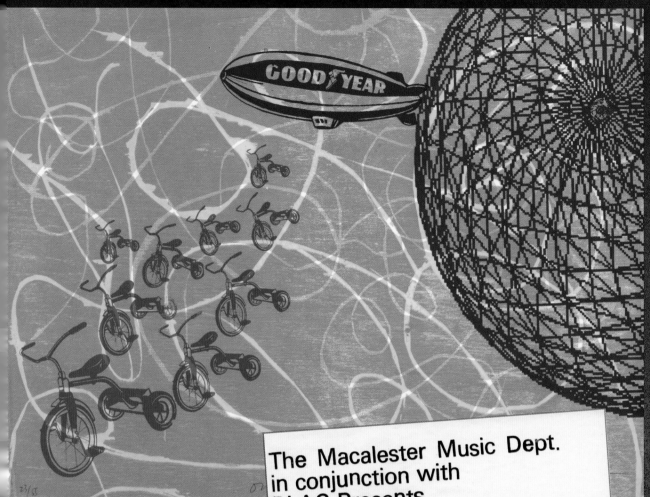

On My Way to Akron, Ohio, an eight-color woodcut with a red strike screenprint by Hui Chu Ying, also includes the Goodyear blimp, an icon of the old rubber industry based in that city, and a molecule ball of polymer, which is the city's new engine of commerce. Photopolymers, light-reactive plastics, can be used to make printing blocks.

Handset letterpress typography forms the basis of this African Drum Ensemble poster. Black and red are selected for graphic impact, but also for thematic ties with the African culture. The word *FREE* is set in a rare example of enameled wood Latin Expanded type from 1887, an early experiment with celluloid-coated letters. French Clarendon Condensed and Universe Sans Serif round out the ensemble of letterforms.

The Macalester Music Dept. in conjunction with BLAC Presents

THE AFRICAN MUSIC ENSEMBLE

directed by Sowah Mensah

with

SAAKUMU

a touring group from Ghana led by Bernard Woma

IN A BLACK HISTORY MONTH CONCERT

FEB.16, 2008 8PM

JANET WALLACE FINE ARTS CENTER

FREE

tickets at the door

A fine woodcut titled *Colorado Morning* by Melanie Yazzie features a self-portrait on her daily walk. The border is her grandmother's traditional Navaho rug pattern, while ancient indigenous petroglyph motifs form part of the figure. A subtle lacey transparent overlay of screenprint ink finishes the design.

Detroit Cobras slither into Vancouver with this great woodcut poster by Sean StarWars. The artist is seriously dedicated to the medium, sticking to a stric schedule of making one woodcut per week for life. *www.seanstarwars.com*

CHAPTER THREE

Digital Printing
and Photocopies

Chester Carlson invented electrophotography equipment with DIY home experiments in 1938. It took until 1959, however, for the Haloid Photographic Company in Rochester, New York, to make commercially viable machines from Carlson's invention. Haloid became Xerox in 1961. As photocopying grew increasingly common and affordable, *Life*, *Time*, and *National Geographic* magazine imagery began appearing in pop art collages of the 1960s. Collage has since become a time-honored way to make band posters and event announcements.

SPONTANEOUSLY
COMBUSTIBLE

4

The
Scrapyard

Have a
HEART
for the
HOMELESS

benefit sale. live music. July 28, 8pm.

THE BARE ESSENTIALS

- Original images, such as printed photos
- Found paper (a.k.a. ephemera)
- Paper
- Good scissors
- Utility knife
- Tape
- Glue sticks
- Markers
- Pens
- Correction fluid (the kind made for copiers)

More recently, scanners have expanded the ease of borrowing high-resolution images, while color laser printing is readily available at copy shops. But black-and-white photocopies still represent the fastest and cheapest way to make a lot of multiples of an image very inexpensively. Copy machines can be found secondhand, but making nice with your local late-night copy center clerk is also a fine idea.

Where to Get Imagery

Sourcing your images from high-quality printed products is a good idea (see discussion of copyright issues). While you can find lots of cool images on the web, there is a problem with most images posted to the internet: many are 72 ppi (pixels per inch), which look great on the screen, but are absolutely terrible for most printing processes. If you need to resize the picture larger, you will notice the images become pixelated into little blocks and lose detail.

Small but mighty, the strong spiral motif against a random pattern really pops in this Walt Mink mini flyer. Fitting for a band named after a professor of psychology. *Designers: John Kimbrough and Candice Belanoff*

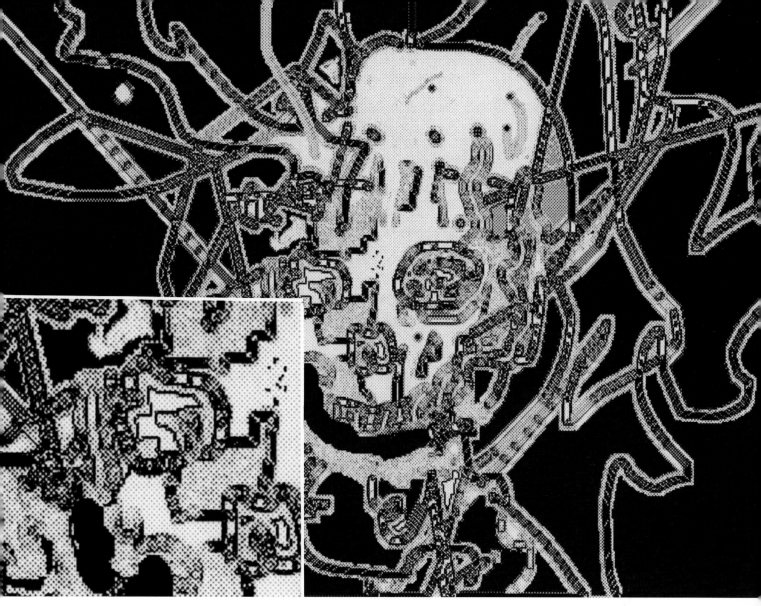

Internet graphics are usually 72 dpi, which look great on the screen, but result in pixelated, blocky images. For printed graphics, 300 dpi is the minimum; 600 dpi or higher results in even more detail. Use a scanner or higher setting on a digital camera for source images. Resolution of photos from inexpensive cellphones will be too low. In the early days of computer graphics, all digital images were a bit blocky, like this vintage product of an Apple IIsi.

Many internet search engines (including Google and Bing) allow you to parse out images of higher resolution. Better yet, get your images from sources other than the web. For example, find old photographs at yard sales and thrift shops, scan them out of books or magazines, and take digital photos at higher megabyte settings (which will translate into higher resolution). Such found imagery is often referred to as ephemera. Or draw your own images or find an artist willing to trade comps to your next show or a CD for their work.

A Word about Copyright Issues

If you are making an item for sale, such as a CD or T-shirt, borrowing someone else's images without their permission can get you in trouble. This could include anything from fines to orders to have all your merchandise destroyed. That could be really bad news. But if you think about it, you want images unique to your product anyway. If you must use found images on merchandise for resale, do it in a way that makes it clear you are not trying to profit from someone else's recognizable and protected photo or image. There's often a thin line between artistic satire that is fair use (a form of protected speech) and ripping off the work of others. And defending oneself in court is expensive.

THE DANCING CIGARETTES

from Bloomington Indiana   On Tour Summer 82

Torn paper recopied after it is collaged. Recopying creates abstract shapes from the figures of the band the Dancing Cigarettes. Many of the band members were also skilled artists. This postcard announced one of their tours. *Artist: Michael Gitlin*

Making the Original

Lay out your collage on a piece of clean backing paper before you glue it down. Rearrange for the best composition. Squint to check for readability. Once glued, try pinning it up and stand across the room to see if it will read on a phone pole or from a car. Since some photocopy machines and printers don't print all the way to the edge, it is good to leave a little margin, up to half an inch all around your design.

TIP

Put another set of eyes on the job. Have a friend proofread your text to make sure your band name is spelled right, the address is accurate, and you have the correct date and time. Consider adding some contact info, too. Nothing like starting a flash mob by mistake.

A birthday card collage makes good use of torn and cut paper, magazine photos, Wite-Out, and metallic markers. The artist paid attention to the use of varying size/scale, as well as black and white and vivid color. *Artist: Valerie Taylor*

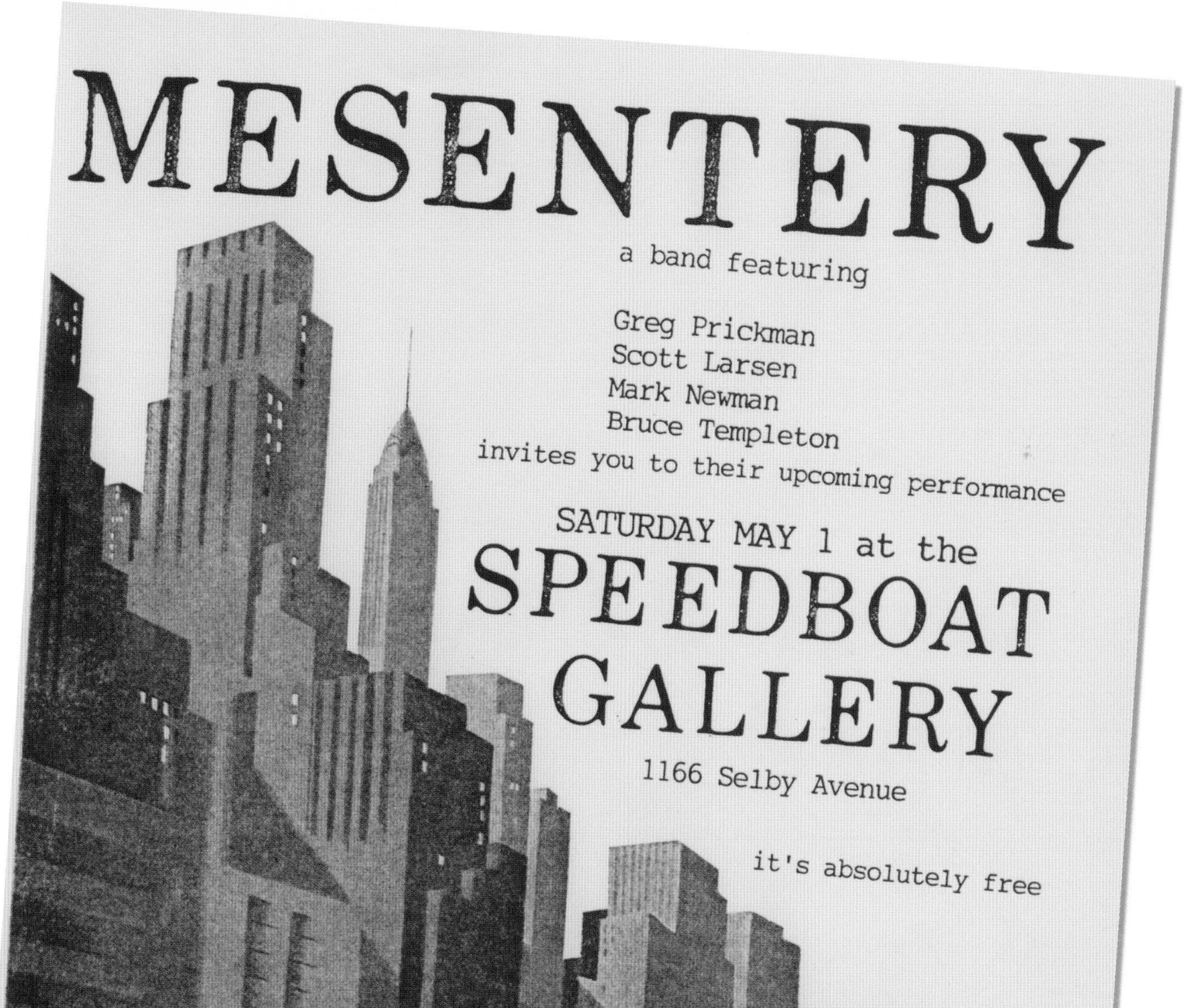

MESENTERY

a band featuring

Greg Prickman
Scott Larsen
Mark Newman
Bruce Templeton
invites you to their upcoming performance

SATURDAY MAY 1 at the

SPEEDBOAT GALLERY

1166 Selby Avenue

it's absolutely free

This black-and-white photocopy on cream-colored paper has a great stylish retro feel to it. Vintage images, antique wood type, and typewriter text are photocopied together seamlessly. Off-white papers, such as antique white, cream, or ivory, help reinforce the concept of nostalgia. *Artist: Greg Prickman*

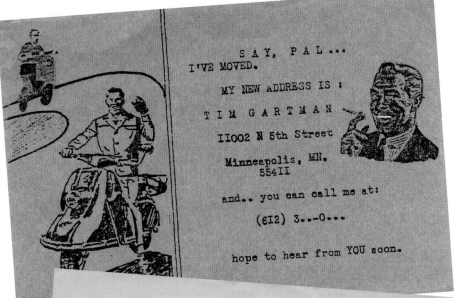

SAY, PAL...
I'VE MOVED.
MY NEW ADDRESS IS :
T I M   G A R T M A N
11002 N 5th Street
Minneapolis, MN.
55411
and.. you can call me at:
(612) 3..-0...
hope to hear from YOU soon.

Typewriters, like Vespas, can have great retro appeal, evoking a different graphic voice. In his lifetime, Tim Gartman hung onto all kinds of antique machinery (including printing presses) and kept them in running condition. This dashing moving notice is not only photocopied on bright blue paper, but also finished with a tiny touch of white colored pencil on the eyeballs and teeth. Numbers have been changed to protect current residents. *Author collection*

Photocopying

A photocopier can yield very effective graphic images. Good high-contrast black-and-white graphics can grab the attention of your audience with the added advantage of being extremely inexpensive to make. Copy shops in major cities are open 24 hours a day, while the advent of computer processes have made it possible to find small good-quality black-and-white copiers at yard sales and going-out-of-business sales.

Photocopy technology works with the aid of static electricity. A static charge is built up on a metal drum inside the machine. Toner—made from a fine metallic sand, such as black iron oxide—is made to hold an opposite charge. A bright lamp reflects off the white areas of the image to be copied as it is face down on the glass. The reflected light affects the charge on the drum, and toner sticks only to the oppositely charged areas in the exact pattern of the original design. Thus

TRANSYLVANIA!

Recital of East-European Music

BILL SCHWARZ · MIRIAM STURM

Friday Sept. 7 IMU Craftshop
8 PM Mezzanine Floor - Union Bldg.

Contrasting paper color with strong, high-contrast graphics can catch a viewer's attention. If the flyer will be folded, be sure to check where the crease will hit the images so it looks good both open and folded shut. This handbill for a recital by Bill Schwarz and violin virtuoso Miriam Sturm also has cute costumed-kid appeal.

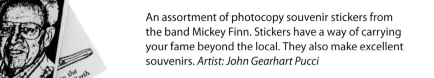

An assortment of photocopy souvenir stickers from the band Mickey Finn. Stickers have a way of carrying your fame beyond the local. They also make excellent souvenirs. *Artist: John Gearhart Pucci*

Chester Carlson, inventor of the Xerox machine, made it onto a postage stamp. Why not mail some posters, flyers, or postcards? Be sure to use stamps with related themes or interesting graphics.

Sometimes good things come in small packages. This small but awesome photocopy sticker for the band Perplexa was created by Jenny Schmid, bassist for this group featured on Detroit's Small Stone Recordings.

Die-cut CD labels designed for use in copiers and laser printers have peel-off backings and get you out of cutting each one by hand. Find them in office supply stores and online.

electrophotography, a.k.a. photocopying, is really a form of stenciling using electricity and light. A device called a corona discharger, very much like a piece of tinsel, sweeps over the paper, readying it for the electrostatically charged toner to hop on and cling tight until it is fused with heat and spit out of the machine.

If you are using a black-and-white copier, make sure the machine prints a dark, rich black and has a good supply of toner. For color copies, which are expensive, check to see that the colors are printing the way you want; some colors don't reproduce well, while some machines are badly calibrated and mess with your color output. Whether you're making black or color copies, run a test before you commit to a lot of copies.

Color papers can really add to the graphic impact of a black photocopy. Select colors that add to the mood and message you want to convey. A good selection is available specifically for copiers. On the downside, color stock is slightly more expensive and may run and fade if exposed to the elements.

TIP

Never try to run regular plastic through a copier or laser printer. It can melt inside the hot machine and wreck it. Stick to heat-stable plastics made specifically for the copier, inkjet, or laser printer being used. Check the packaging carefully.

Stickers are another popular way to spread your message and they make nice souvenirs. Most copiers can take sticker paper. Avery brand labels with peel-off backing come in full sheets designed to go through printers. Avery also makes die-cut CD labels designed for use in copiers and laser printers. They can be found online and in office supply stores.

If you print stickers, familiarize yourself with the hand-feed slot on the copier. It is usually a fold-down flap on the side of the machine. Heavy paper and sticker stock are fed one at a time into the slot instead of via the bulk tray so they don't jam inside the machine. You may want to send a plain piece of paper marked with an X through the hand-feed slot first so you can check which side of the sticker paper should go face up. Once printed, try preserving stickers with overspray varnish, available from art supply stores, or with hairspray from a drugstore so they don't disintegrate as rapidly in the rain. This treatment is especially good for bumper stickers, which get a lot of abuse. Some art and craft stores sell an amazing array of printable sticker stock, from fluorescent neon colors to glossy sparkly paper. Both clear and translucent sticker paper is available for novel graphic effects. See-through stickers go well on windows and plastic CD covers. Copy machines often have media settings that allow the machine to make subtle adjustments to the way it grips the paper as well as the amount of toner used, so check to see if the setting should be changed from plain paper to transparency, cardstock, heavy paper, or the like. A better print will result.

Fancy art-quality papers, such as linen, cotton fiber, and preprinted stock, are available precut, designed to go through photocopy machines and laser printers. A limited amount of fancier papers made for résumés and greeting cards are available at copy centers. Art stores will have a larger supply. Not all art paper can go through a copy machine, but a surprising variety can, including Rives lightweight, Strathmore, Bristol, and Canson papers. Some translucent vellum papers also work well. Consult art supply store personnel for their recommendations. Look for smooth, lighter-weight stock. Don't try to send bricks through the copier. You can get large sheets of art paper and cut them down yourself, but I would only advise doing this if you have access to a very accurate paper cutter. The gripper strips on copy machines can be quite touchy and may reject miscut paper or, worse, wad it up and jam inside. However, paper jams are not the end of the world. Simply turn the machine off, open it up, pull out the stuck paper, shut the machine firmly until its latches click, and turn it back on. Look closely at the next photocopier you encounter. Located just inside the fold-down flaps and doors are handy little numbered and color-coded pictograms showing how to load paper, change trays, open the machine, switch out toner cartridges, and unjam paper. Most of the levers inside are color-coded, too, to help the repair person on unfamiliar models. One DIY theory is if a human made it, a human can figure out how to fix it.

Transfer paper made for copiers is available from some office supply stores and is used for ironing on T-shirts, with varying results. This might be a useful option if you need only one or two shirts on short notice—screenprinting is always the recommended process for printing on multiple shirts. Wash any new T-shirt before trying to affix an image to it. This will remove starches and chemicals used in the manufacturing process and help the image stay in the fabric.

it is the ambiguous gesture which interests us.

Photocopies with dramatically degenerated visuals sometimes pack a graphic punch. This postcard uses a pair of dark figures submerged in static to invoke a love of ambiguity. Recopying copies degrades the detail but amplifies the noise—akin to creating feedback and distortion with musical instruments.
Artist: Michael Gitlin

ART ATTACK GALLERY

dip

PETROGLYPH PAINTINGS BY DAVID D'ANDRADE

Petroglyph Paintings by David D'Andrade was an exhibit promoted via a postcard with the scraped and scrawled feel of stark, high-contrast copier effects on contrasting turquoise paper. *Courtesy Art Attack Gallery, San Francisco*

Paper Sizes and Weights Worldwide

Typical precut printer paper sizes in North America are letter (8.5x11 inches), legal (8.5x14), and tabloid (also called ledger, 11x17). Postcard sizes are 3.5x5 and 4.25x6 inches. At the start of larger paper sizes is super B (13x19), sometimes called A+ and often seen in photo-quality papers made for inkjet printers. Many copy shops offer oversize prints, but not in the self-service areas. Art prints on archival watercolor paper up to 24x36 inches can look wonderful. Big banners up to 4x10 feet are also available for a price. Some shops have a cheaper black-and-white big printer for architectural plans. Ask

to see samples of the output so you have an idea of what you'll get for your money. Printing extra-large sizes often takes time and is not usually available at the spur of the moment, so plan ahead. Shops can also mount and laminate posters on foamboard, which is great for an outdoor marquee or a protest march in the rain. You can order signs printed on corrugated plastic sheets, PVC plastic, or even metal—in store or online—and the prices are fairly reasonable for such a permanent product. Generally, you work at the copy center on time-rented computers with graphics programs or you bring in a laptop or flash drive with your file, or in some cases send a file from a mobile device.

A ream of paper is 500 sheets, which is the way you'll see it packaged in a copy center. The weight of paper, or more precisely its density, is referred to in pounds per ream, but of a stack of 17x22-inch sheets. The higher the number, the thicker or heavier the paper will be. Thus a standard pack of 500 sheets of normal copy paper is fairly lightweight in its 20-pound classification. Its gram weight will be listed as 75gsm/10M. In contrast, cardstock weighs in at a beefy 50 to 110 pounds. Should you ever deal with paper manufacturers or try to get a bulk paper deal from a factory that makes paper, the first question they might ask is what weight of paper you are looking for. Several manufacturers' websites, such as French Paper (www.frenchpaper.com) and Mohawk (www.mohawkconnects.com), offer good explanations of these issues.

In Europe and most of the rest of the world (except the United States and Canada), the standard paper sizes, using the ISO system, have a completely different scheme. For example, a basic sheet called A4 is 210x297 millimeters, which is about 8.27x11.69 inches. Walk into a copy shop on your European tour and you may have to alter the size of your poster's graphics.

Mess Up Your Photocopies

Since photocopies are cheap, if you have access to a machine for an extended period of time, you can play with unusual effects. A photocopier will try its best to print images as it perceives them. But nothing is more human than pushing at the boundaries of what machines can do, and really, these machines are only

Greg Metz gave himself a "Hoosierectomy" when he left Indiana for Texas. He used degenerated photocopy effects to mimic noisy static on a television screen. *www.gregmetzartstudio.com*

minimally perceptive. Notice that the scanning lamp on a photocopier goes by at a relatively slow pace. You can take an image and drag it just off pace from the light, sometimes with quite surreal results as the image bends and lengthens. Think of Salvador Dali's melted watches.

You can also send a photocopy through the machine twice, making for twinned or double-printed images. Be sure the image has dried and the paper has cooled before sending it through again. Check to see which side of the paper should be up when you send it back through. Static may build up on the printed surface and tend to curl the paper up. Lay it face down and weight it with a book, stack of paper, or something heavy until it relaxes.

Many computer graphics effects were derived from early experiments with copy machines. Lightening or darkening the brightness and contrast in Photoshop is the equivalent of changing the toner density settings on a copier. Normally images that are too light are considered poor quality. But that ephemeral look may be what you're after. Play with the image density buttons or sliders to see what you can get in the "barely there" category. Printing a first ghostlike image with subsequent over-copying in rich black can look great.

If you've ever gotten a printed school lab handout, you know that after a while reprints of reprints degrade in detail and quality. But Photoshop has a photocopy filter for just this type of grainy outcome, so why not make that effect yourself? Taking a crisp image

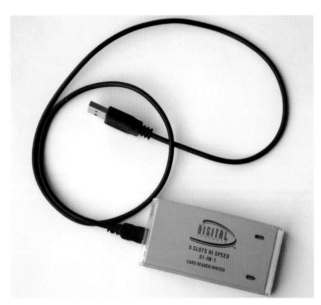

You can buy a very inexpensive card reader device at an electronics store. It accepts several digital camera card formats, making it a handy universal translator.

and repeatedly copying the copies eventually gives a somewhat organic pixelation pattern. The same is true of continual blowups. Try scaling up pictures in size percentage until they disintegrate into random dots and noise. Decay can be quite beautiful.

Digital Imaging

If you have access to a scanner, a computer with graphics software, and a digital printer, you are in business as a desktop print shop. Photoshop is great but expensive software. You can actually do some effective layout and design with a Word program, but its ability to manipulate images is limited.

Image manipulation with computer graphics software, such as Photoshop, takes some practice. There are fine online tutorials, plus how-to books available at the library and for purchase. Finding a friend, fan, or bandmate with graphics design chops is good, but learning how to do it yourself is better.

Scanning is often the first step in creating a digital image. With practice it becomes obvious which types of collage materials scan well or poorly. While you can use a scanner just like a photocopier, it is more common to scan collaged elements separately and use software such

as Photoshop to assemble the design. There's a reason graphics programs have cut and paste buttons—they come from the art of collage.

A digital camera is a form of scanner; set the file or megabyte size high for best results. Load the images onto your computer's hard drive using the camera's USB cable. Rename your files from image-number-whatever to something descriptive, such as "blue guitar" so they're easier to find and work with.

If your computer has slots, the same task can be accomplished just by inserting the camera chip into the appropriate slot. You can also buy an inexpensive card reader that connects multiple card formats to a computer with a camera cable. It is a handy type of universal translator. Your cellphone may not take very high-resolution images, but if it does, e-mail them to yourself and download them onto your hard drive.

Next, open a new document in your application and size it according to the paper you will print on. This will be your clean "piece of paper" on which you assemble your images and text. Import scanned graphics or cut and paste them using the tools your program provides to place, resize, rotate, and arrange these elements as needed.

Scanning images involves size and resolution considerations. If you scan items at 100 percent size and a very high resolution, your files can be enormous, sometimes too big to fit on a flash drive, in addition to taking forever to print. On the other hand, scanning things at too low a resolution results in poor-quality pixelated pictures. For images appearing on the Internet, 72 ppi is suitable. However, it's terrible for prints on paper. One rule of thumb is to scan items at about double the dpi of the device you will print from. For example, it is common to find a home inkjet or laser printer producing prints at 300 dpi, so scan images for such printers at 600 dpi.

Graphics software is quite expensive, but student discounts are available. You can also check out your local library or see if there's a graphics collective in your community. Or start one.

Saving files as you work on them is very important. Stop frequently in your work and hit the save button in case your application unexpectedly quits or your computer shuts down. Make several backups by saving files to flash drives, DVDs, or a cloud system. Nothing is more frustrating than working for hours on a wonderful design only to have the flash drive go through the wash in your jeans pocket, erasing the only copy of your work. Computer theft is also a fairly common way to lose image files. Duplicating versions of the document as you go and renaming them provides proofs of the stages and changes it went through. Although some graphics programs let you step back a considerable number of steps, sometimes it's good to compare an early version with later ones.

Familiarize yourself with the hand-feed slot on the copier you're using. Send through a plain piece of paper marked with an X on the topside to confirm which side of the sticker paper should go face up. Plain paper is inexpensive compared to stickers and other specialty paper, so it's a worthwhile practice.

The hand-feed slot on a laser printer is used for stickers, heavy paper, and transparencies. Change the paper settings in the Print dialog box on the computer as needed. Sometimes the setting is buried in the pull-down menus, so look carefully at the available options. Also check the color/quality options. The econo mode should be changed to highest quality to print rich blacks and color toners.

Laser printers produce more long-lasting images than inkjet printers do because the toner is waterproof. Home black-and-white laser printers are fairly affordable, and color laser printers have come down in price considerably in recent years. The toner, however, is rather expensive because you need to buy at least the four basic colors used in process printing: cyan, magenta, yellow, and black (together known as CMYK). High-end color printers use several kinds of black toner, such as photo black, as well as shades of the CMYK colors, such as light cyan and light magenta. Some color inkjet printers require nine different toner cartridges and sadly refuse to budge if just one of them is out. Since there isn't an all-night toner aisle at the neighborhood convenience store, it's wise to overstock a supply of cartridges when readying to print. Recycling programs for toner cartridges are increasingly available at office supply stores and keep the plastic waste down.

You may wish to invest in specialty laser printer papers, found in art and office supply stores. These papers can be glossy (often used for high-quality photos), slightly textured, transparent, translucent, or heavyweight, such as cardstock. As discussed in the photocopying section, sticker paper is also available and can be used with the hand-feed slot on a laser printer, similar to those found on copy machines. Triple check transparency labeling for compatibility with the machine in use. The wrong plastic can melt inside the works. Laser-print transfer paper is also available for applying digital images to T-shirts, with the same mixed results as copier transfers. Download and print out a manual for your printer—it can be invaluable. Learn how to clear a paper jam by turning off the machine, opening it, and following instructions found inside the flaps and drawers.

Halftones

Look closely at a printed photograph in a newspaper, magazine, or book. Chances are it will be composed of tiny dots. If you've ever found a torn fragment of a billboard picture, it will be composed of rather large printed dots, usually in the four basic CMYK colors. A nondigital photographic print (made in a darkroom) most often is produced with continuous tone—no dots. The dots used in printing are a way to translate the scale of white-to-gray-to-black in a photo so it can be reliably printed. This is called

Halftone dots add to the grainy black-and-white angst of *The Duluth EP* announcement postcard from Vinnie and the Stardusters. *Designer: Jeaneen Gauthier/ www.jeaneengauthier.com; courtesy Eric Dregni*

halftoning. A black-and-white photo with halftone spots can be printed in just one color of black, but appear to have a full range of subtle grays, an illusion created by the gradation in size of the tiny black dots, giving the appearance of density or sparseness. It is a form of mechanical pixelation. Used by itself, as in Photoshop with a color halftone filter, it gives a kind of retro '60s feel to a design. That's because screenprint graphics of the Pop Art era used exaggerated, highly visible dots to mimic comic books and the Sunday funny papers. Artists like Roy Lichtenstein helped the Ben-Day dot screen (a sheet of dots overlaid on graphics to give them shading) invade the fine-art world, and the look permeated much of the music graphics of the era.

Not every image looks great with a posterized or super high-contrast effect, although Andy Warhol made it his trademark look. Photo stencil screenprinters often need to convert images to halftone in order to keep details accurate when printing. The making of positive transparencies for photo screenprinting is discussed in Chapter 4, but since halftoning is also useful for retaining detail and tones of gray in photocopy designs, here are some techniques to try.

In Photoshop, create an image and select all or part of that image; then pull down Image, choose Mode, and change the selection to Bitmap. Normally digital designers don't care for bitmapped images. They look crude and boxy, but that is the effect you are after in this case. In Bitmap mode, a dialog box will open asking for Resolution Output in pixels per inch. Too fine

PETŐFI CSARNOK
B U D A P E S T

David Byrne

Monster In
The Mirror Tour

In Concert

JÚLIUS 1.

PETŐFI CSARNOK
B U D A P E S T

Lópici Reklám
Budapest

Posters are often "liberated" from telephone poles because someone admires the graphics. Halftone dots add texture to the alien photo image of David Byrne on this handbill announcing a concert stop in Budapest. Black-and-white high-contrast work (i.e., no dots) is called line art, which forms the positive and negative blocks of texts in this example. *Lópici Reklám/Tiny Horse Publicity*

a resolution means the dots won't be visible, which is undesirable for this effect. Try resolutions between 100 and 500. The box also requests specifying the Method, which should be Halftone Screen. Hit OK. The Halftone Screen box opens, requesting a Frequency of lines per inch. The lower the frequency, the bigger the dots. If you are preparing a transparency for screenprinting, try 100 lines per inch. Otherwise, experiment with different numbers until you find a desirable graphic effect. The shape of the dots should usually be round, but sometimes it's fun to try ellipses or the other available shapes. The angle should be set to 45 degrees. Hit OK. Save. Print out a copy on paper before committing to expensive art papers or transparency materials.

Another way to halftone with Photoshop is more specifically useful to creating black and clear transparencies for screenprinting. Use a source image of 300 dpi (dots per inch) or more. Use a digital camera on high-resolution settings to get this image or a flatbed scanner set to 300 dpi or higher. Do not use an image off the web—most are only 72 ppi and quite small. They may look fine on a screen, but printouts will be disastrously inadequate and not translate well or have enough detail for making prints. Pay attention to the print size dimensions for this process. Try to scan or save the image at 100 percent of the size you will ultimately print it in inches. In Photoshop, open or import your image. Select Image Size from Resize in the Image drop-down menu and change the resolution to 1200. If the image blows up out of sight, select View and Fit on Screen. Next select Image, Mode, Grayscale (it's OK to discard the color information), then Image, Adjustments, Brightness/Contrast. Adjust the Contrast slider +30 or more. Select Image, Mode, Bitmap again, and an output of 120, then Method, Halftone Screen. Hit OK. Set the angle at 52.5 degrees and the Frequency at 90 to 100 lines per inch. Select the Round pattern for the Dot Screen and save. Print a black-and-white copy to see if it looks OK.

Performance Graphics

A trend in the Internet community, crossed with the recent crafting craze, is the downloadable print-it-yourself graphic. These fun projects are interactive in nature and leave it to the user to accept the responsibility to manifest the digital and virtual into the material and physical world. Users are requested to download and print out the PDFs, cut, paste, and glue as directed, and they are often urged to snap photos of the results and upload them back to the home site for sharing. Artist Imin Yeh has created The Art of Downloadable Craft website (www.adcsource.com) dedicated as "your source for distractions." Her projects include print-your-own cubicle wallpaper and a paper mahjong set (some, well, a lot of assembly required). Simultaneously witty and critical, her projects address the authenticity of ethnic kitsch via send-ups of Chinese imports. The medium opens possibilities for reaching a new audience and engaging them in playful exchange.

Messing with the Scanner

Scanners, like photocopy machines, try their darnedest to record faithful information as they see it. It is your job as a human to mess with their little machine brains. Try getting one step ahead of the scanning light for a cascading river of pixels. Reflective items are particularly perplexing to the digital mind. Try scanning textured cloth, plastic wrap, aluminum foil, tinsel, a mirror ball, squished plastic packaging, wrinkled paper, toys, tools . . . the possibilities are endless. Like some medieval paintings, an item can appear early on the scanning glass, disappear, and reappear later. The goal of these types of games is to come up with a more unique look. Graphics programs have a stock set of effects and filters, but sometimes it is fun to come up with something outside the box for your source material. Three-dimensional objects from the real world sometimes look surprising smushed up against the scanning glass, although the scanning of body parts is a bit cliché. If you are going to scan unusual objects, especially if they are moist, dirty, particulate (like sand or glitter), or organic, or if they might scratch the glass, first lay down an intermediate sheet of clear acetate or Mylar. The scanner won't notice it, and you won't wreck the glass for when it needs to make clean scans.

Print, cut out scalloped edges. Make

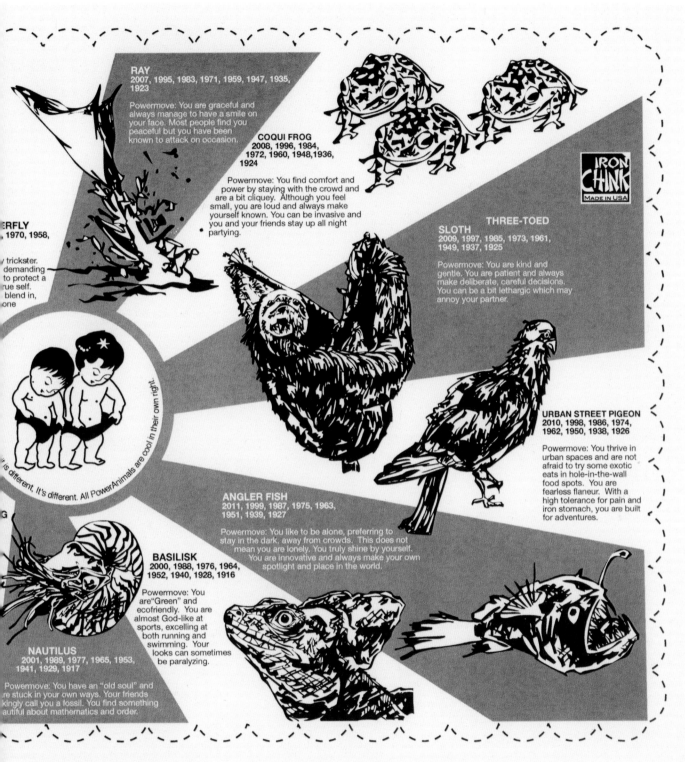

RAY
2007, 1995, 1983, 1971, 1959, 1947, 1935, 1923

Powermove: You are graceful and always manage to have a smile on your face. Most people find you peaceful but you have been known to attack on occasion.

COQUI FROG
2008, 1996, 1984, 1972, 1960, 1948, 1936, 1924

Powermove: You find comfort and power by staying with the crowd and are a bit cliquey. Although you feel small, you are loud and always make yourself known. You can be invasive and you and your friends stay up all night partying.

...ERFLY
..., 1970, 1958,

...y trickster. ...demanding ...to protect a ...rue self. ...blend in, ...one

THREE-TOED SLOTH
2009, 1997, 1985, 1973, 1961, 1949, 1937, 1925

Powermove: You are kind and gentle. You are patient and always make deliberate, careful decisions. You can be a bit lethargic which may annoy your partner.

URBAN STREET PIGEON
2010, 1998, 1986, 1974, 1962, 1950, 1938, 1926

Powermove: You thrive in urban spaces and are not afraid to try some exotic eats in hole-in-the-wall food spots. You are fearless flaneur. With a high tolerance for pain and iron stomach, you are built for adventures.

...s different. It's different. All PowerAnimals are cool in their own right.

ANGLER FISH
2011, 1999, 1987, 1975, 1963, 1951, 1939, 1927

Powermove: You like to be alone, preferring to stay in the dark, away from crowds. This does not mean you are lonely. You truly shine by yourself. You are innovative and always make your own spotlight and place in the world.

BASILISK
2000, 1988, 1976, 1964, 1952, 1940, 1928, 1916

Powermove: You are "Green" and ecofriendly. You are almost God-like at sports, excelling at both running and swimming. Your looks can sometimes be paralyzing.

NAUTILUS
2001, 1989, 1977, 1965, 1953, 1941, 1929, 1917

Powermove: You have an "old soul" and ...re stuck in your own ways. Your friends ...kingly call you a fossil. You find something ...autiful about mathematics and order.

IRON CHINK
MADE IN USA

...ous meal, place on top, snap a picture and send it to ADCsource.com. Enjoy the food!

An internet trend crossed with the recent crafting craze is the downloadable print-it-yourself graphic. Users download and print out PDFs, then cut, paste, and glue as directed. Artist Imin Yeh's witty and critical projects, such as her *Poweranimal Placemats to Eat On*, address the authenticity of ethnic kitsch via sendups of Chinese imports. *www.iminyeh.info*

Robert Davis made the covers for his CD, *Olsen Twinns*, from color laser copies, recycled cereal boxes, and graphics by Lily Parmenter and Marlys Mandaville. It was an intensive labor of love for an independently produced product.

Daniel Clinton-McCausland used color laser copies and made the CD covers for Phantom Vibrations out of hand cut recycled corrugated cardboard.

A Dancing Cigarettes 7-inch picture sleeve designed by the author. Found objects were laid on the copier with the contrast turned way up.

Opposite: This Maiden Rock Revue event poster has classic black-and-white graphic impact. Maiden Rock is a tiny picturesque Wisconsin river burg. Trains come whistling through town several times a day, headed down tracks alongside the Mississippi. *Artist: David Wyrick*

Maiden Rock Revue
T R A I N S
MUSIC • VISUAL ART • SPOKEN WORD
Hosted By
The DitchLilies and Celeste Nelms
with Special Guests
B.J. Christofferson • Emily Huppert
Michelle Meyer • DJ Rock Crusher
Saturday May 23, 2009
Maiden Rock American Legion Post
$10 per person   doors at 7:00 show at 8:00   cash bar   no pets

Vintage photocopy poster for an all-ages show at Speedboat Gallery/Motor Oil Coffee Shop in St. Paul, Minnesota. *Artist: John Gearhart Pucci*

SPEEDBOAT GALLERY

647-9733

1166 SELBY SAINT PAUL

MOTOR OIL

BIKINI KILL SMUT
GODHEAD SILO
SUNDAY SEPTEMBER 20
ALL AGES. NO BOOZE.

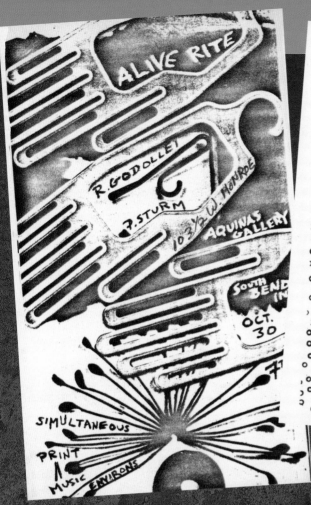

The idea of something futuristic is relative. I used the wrapping paper from a mimeograph machine for this high-contrast photocopy postcard design. Part of the Sputnik and Telstar generation, the graphic implied far-off fantasies of space travel not yet realized.

This postcard advertises a print/music environs, entitled Alive Rite, between myself and electronic musician Paul Sturm. The image was created by laying odd found objects, including vintage ladies' glove drying hangers, on the photocopy glass. Hand-lettering was applied in the recopying phase. The announcement was printed economically four-up on cardstock, cut in quarters, and mailed at the inexpensive postcard rate.

What Would Hüsker Dü?

In the late 1980s Minneapolis photographer Daniel Corrigan (www.danielcorrigan.com) created photocopied paper stickers cleverly playing on the name of the recently disbanded Hüsker Dü. In 2010, Voyageur Press re-created vinyl versions for inclusion in their biography of the band.

This terrific color laser print flyer for The Bike Comics Show was a collaboration. Roger Lootine started it with a self-portrait (right). He e-mailed it to Ken Avidor, who added the drawing of himself battling an octopus. Avidor e-mailed it to Andy Singer, who portrayed himself and the bicycle trailer flying overhead, colored the image, and laid it out in Photoshop using the overused but still good Comics Sans typeface.

Featuring bicycle cartoons and drawings by Ken Avidor, Roger Lootine and Andy Singer.

www.bikewalkweek.org   www.saintpaulbicyclecoalition.org

Rich Black designs unforgettable pulp fiction/comic book graphic–style posters for rock bands such as Devotchka, Elvis Costello, Maroon 5, and the Misfits. His rousing Occupy Oakland poster is downloadable through Occuprint, which collects, prints, and distributes posters from the worldwide Occupy movement. Occupy has generated some extraordinarily compelling graphics. *Courtesy www.occuprint.org by permission of the artist*

This fine black-and-white letter-size photocopy poster announces a multiband lineup at St. Paul's Speedboat Gallery in 1988. Scott Dolan did all the illustrations and text by hand, with the exception of a typed phone number. It's a complete package and the graphics let you know what kind of show you are in for: original, stripped-down, indie-punk fun. Speedboat operated an alternative-art gallery upstairs, providing cover for the illegal rock shows in the basement.

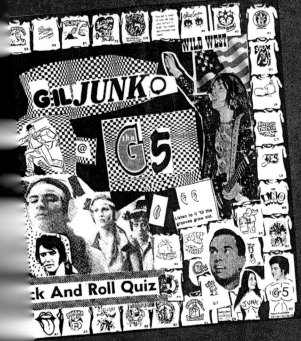

The Glenrustles were a stalwart outfit on the 1990s Minneapolis rock scene. This 7-inch sleeve featured a woodcut by local artist Bruce Mann depicting John the Baptist's head on a platter. The original woodcut was then photocopied three-up on 22x17 sheets of various colors. The resulting sleeves were trimmed and folded in half to wrap around premade plain paper sleeves holding the records. The works were then inserted in a plastic sleeve. The rustic woodcut medium worked well with the band's ragged roots-rock aesthetic, especially when degenerated a bit by the photocopy process. *www.richmattsonmusic.com*

Mark Lindquist of Shaky Ray Records out of Duluth, Minnesota, employed a simple cut, paste, and photocopy technique for the sleeve of this G5/Giljunko split EP to create a sense of old-school punk rock raunch.

Founded in 2000 by Xavier Tavera and Douglas Padilla, Grupo Soap del Corazon is a group of Latino artists and allies hosting exhibits and projects. Member Luis Fitch of Uno Hispanic Branding (*www.unoonline.com*) designed the distinctive black-on-red El Milagro image, which Padilla and Tavera had screenprinted as posters and made into photocopy handbills.

CHAPTER FOUR

Screen-printing

Screenprint technology developed as an improvement on the basic principle of stenciling. The ancient Chinese are said to have stretched horsehair across an open stencil to prolong its usefulness, since repeatedly daubing ink across a paper stencil causes it to curl up. Screenprinters today stretch a mesh of fabric tightly across a frame, apply a stencil to one side, and use a squeegee to scrape ink across the stencil, through the mesh, and onto the paper or fabric to be printed. Printers no longer use silk for the mesh, as polyester monofilament (think fishing line) is sturdier and more waterproof. A separate screen stencil must normally be made for each color the artist wishes to print. Each color is usually run (printed) in a large quantity before changing the stencil and printing the next color.

THE BARE ESSENTIALS

- Screen with frame
- Squeegee
- Ink
- Paper
- Long-blade spatula or paint-stirring stick
- Masking tape
- Duct tape
- Transparencies or paper stencils
- Photo emulsion
- Stencil remover
- Quartz exposure light
- Window glass
- Source of running water
- High-pressure hose for cleanup

Optional: wood, miter box, staple gun, and staples for making your own screen frames

Screenprint Methods

Paper Stencils

Paper stencils (see Chapter 1) can be used in conjunction with silkscreens. A distinct advantage of using a screen with a stencil over it, directly printing a stencil, is the image lasts longer, you get more prints, and they are generally better quality. One advantage over photo stencil screen processes (see below) is that no electronic equipment is needed.

After you cut a paper stencil, affix it with masking tape to the print side (bottom) of the screen. It should read correctly (a.k.a. it is "right reading") through the screen from the squeegee (top) side. Print as with other screenprint methods described later in this chapter.

Glue and Blockout Stencils

This is similar to the paper stencil method, except the stencil won't get soggy or wrinkled. Glue or liquid blockout, such as Speedball Screen Filler, is painted onto the screen in negative. In other words, you paint the liquid onto the screen, avoiding those image areas where you want the ink to pass through onto the paper or fabric. You are clogging up the screen fabric where you don't want ink to pass through. Print as with other screenprint methods.

Screen filler, also known as liquid blockout, is painted onto a clean screen to make a stencil, clogging up the screen fabric where you don't want ink to pass through. Screen fillers like those offered by Speedball won't get soggy with several passes of water-based ink, unlike paper stencils. *Bottle courtesy Speedball Art Products®*

Red Toad

5/14

Javier Rodriguez

Photo Screenprint

With this process, the screen basically is coated with a light-sensitive goo (photographic emulsion) and allowed to dry. Exposure to light hardens the emulsion into a durable stencil.

To make a photo screenprint, you first need a positive transparency. Transparencies are sheets of plastic with some black and some clear areas. A transparency such as a photocopy on plastic or a drawing on Mylar is laid on the coated screen before exposure to control where the light will harden the emulsion. Areas on the transparency that are dark will block out the exposure light and prevent the emulsion from hardening. These soft areas will wash out in water, leaving an opening in the stencil for ink to pass through.

Here's a good example of "negative" work using screen filler. *Red Toad* by Javier Rodriguez retains lots of the artist's energetic brushwork. Areas in white were painted with blockout, as was the brushed edge. When squeegeed, red ink skipped the blocked areas and printed in the spaces in between.

Making a Positive Transparency

On a Photocopier

Most high-contrast hand-drawn work can be photocopied and printed out as a plastic transparency at your local copy store. Make two copies and tape them together with clear tape for adequate image density. Most black-and-white copiers have a hand-feed slot where you can load transparencies yourself. However, you must use the correct kind of plastic, one made for your kind of

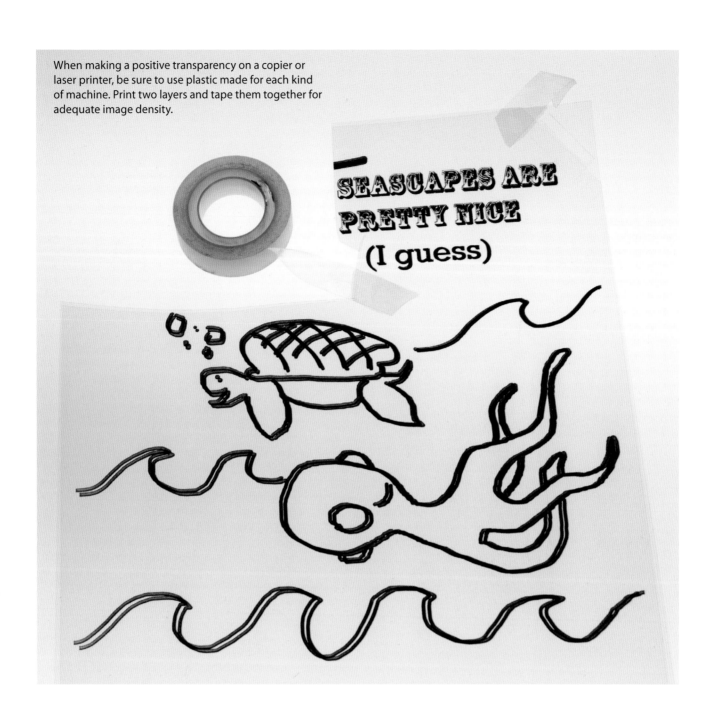

When making a positive transparency on a copier or laser printer, be sure to use plastic made for each kind of machine. Print two layers and tape them together for adequate image density.

photocopy machine. Use of the wrong plastic will melt inside the machine, screw up its works, and possibly cause a fire.

With a Laser Printer

Any hand-drawn work can be scanned, made into a digital file, and printed out as a laser transparency at your local copy store. In addition, computers are particularly good for typing text and resizing it. However, very tiny type might not print well, as small images can clog up the screen mesh (especially if it's too fine) or drop through the mesh (if it's too coarse). Text that is 12-point bold or larger will give a printer the least trouble.

Computers are also useful for laying out images in multiples. Consider designing stickers or postcards to be printed several at a time, such as four, eight, or ten to a sheet to be cut apart later. It saves time and paper. Remember to build in sufficient margins around each image.

Investing in your own black-and-white laser printer, new or used, is fairly affordable. (Inkjet printers are usually not suitable for making transparencies; their ink

is not dense enough.) Most laser printers have a hand-feed slot where you can load transparencies. As with a photocopier, it is very important to use the correct kind of plastic so you don't damage the machine. 3M, Office Max, and HP all offer laser transparencies. Laser-printed plastic, like that printed on a photocopier, should be layered for adequate image density. Print out two copies of your design and tape them together with clear tape. You can hold them up to a window or use a light table to line them up.

Draw by Hand with Opaque Pens

Artists and printers have been known to make transparencies with Sharpie marker images on paper made translucent by a coating of walnut oil, but this method is very messy. Instead, hand draw on a piece of plastic. Unfortunately, even the blackest Sharpie will not be dense enough to hold back the bright light needed to expose the photo emulsion. Buy a specialty opaque pen. Kimoto and RISO make them in a variety of widths and they are available from art supply stores and online.

If you draw your design by hand on Mylar plastic, be sure to use opaque pens. Sharpies and other regular markers won't block out the light needed to expose certain photo emulsions properly.

Professional Transparencies

Large film positives can be made with the help of a service bureau, typically from an uploaded digital file. Service bureaus can make large-size, dense-black transparencies with fine details, but they are not cheap. Layered together, two laser transparencies are about the same density as a professional transparency for a fraction

TIP

It's a good idea to learn how to open your copier or laser printer to retrieve any stuck paper or jammed plastic. While in there, see where new toner cartridges go. Do this with the machine uplugged so you don't get a shock.

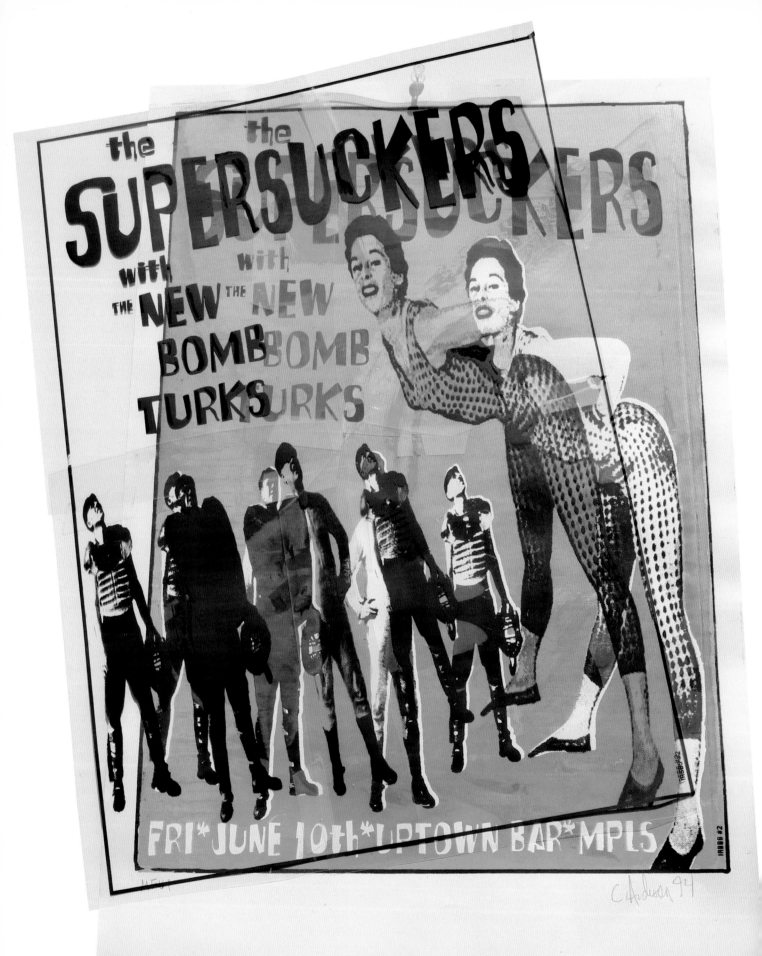

Opposite: Oversize positives can be made by taping several 8.5x11-inch transparencies together. This Supersuckers screenprint poster was an early design including a custom font by Chank Diesel. Warhol-esque use of bright spot color under a black key image gives the poster a retro '60s feel. A variable blend of swipes from lavender to turquoise are under each image. *www.chank.com*

TIP

Avoid cotton organdy for making screens. While inexpensive, it stretches with water-based ink and stains badly.

of the cost. If you decide to go the service bureau route, find one online or in the phone book under the listing "graphic services" or "digital file preparation."

Making a Screen vs. Buying a Premade Screen

To make your own screen, you'll need screenprint fabric, a wooden frame, a staple gun, staples, and a hammer. A miter box for sawing the wood on the diagonal is also helpful, as are friends to stretch fabric while you work the staple gun.

Buy screenprint fabric by the yard online or from an art store. Look for polyester monofilament fabric, between 150 and 250 mesh (a measure of the number of threads per linear inch). Too fine a mesh makes it hard to push ink through the screen, while mesh that is too open, such

as number 50, lets fine details drop through the openings in the fabric. Buy fabric bigger all the way around than your frame, since you need to be able to grasp some extra fabric when you stretch it over the frame.

You will need a wooden frame across which you can stretch the fabric by stapling it down with a staple gun. Buy 2x2-inch wood stock at a lumberyard or home center and cut the ends on the diagonal with a miter saw, as if you were making a picture frame. Fasten together with screws instead of nails, since you'll be using water to rinse out ink and stencils, and wood swells when wet. If possible, buy cedar instead of pine, since it stands up better to water.

Make the frame at least 5 inches larger on every side than the largest work you'll typically print. That means make a screen frame about 20x24 inches if you want to print 8.5x11-inch posters.

If the screen comes with a selvage, a tightly woven border on one side, use that side to begin stapling fabric

If you have access to a woodshop equipped with a chop saw or miter box, you can make your own screen frames by cutting 2x2-inch lumber (cedar is a good water-resistant choice) on a 45-degree angle and using screws (not nails) to assemble the frames. Keep frames as flat as possible. Avoid cheap premade screens with corrugated metal fasteners—they rust and bust. Screenprint supply houses in larger cities sell professional wood and aluminum premade screens at reasonable rates.

TIP

Discarded screens can sometimes be scavenged from the dumpsters of professional screenprinting shops. It won't hurt to ask first if you can have them. Slice off any old fabric with a razor blade and pull up old staples with pliers.

Water-based photo emulsions typically come in two parts: a container of goo and a bottle of sensitizer. *Courtesy Speedball Art Products®*

to the frame. Otherwise, center fabric over the frame with extra material hanging over on all sides. Tack down the fabric making a row of staples about 1 inch apart. Stapling diagonally instead of perpendicular or parallel to the frame will reduce tears and runs in the screen. Have friends pull the fabric by grabbing the excess on opposite sides of the frame as you tack to make a nice, tightly stretched screen. Use the edge of the frame for leverage to help pull the fabric tight. Continue to pull in cross directions as you staple along the sides until the whole screen is tacked down. Now is the chance to pry up any misplaced staples with a screwdriver or the handy tack puller on the back of some staple guns. Pulling the fabric extra hard, go around the entire screen again, stapling in between each previous staple, smoothing out any wrinkles as you go. Once the screen is stretched tightly like a drum, hammer down the staples. A quarter should be able to bounce off the finished screen.

Buying a premade screen is an excellent option for those not particularly handy with tools. Premade screens can be found at art supply stores. Avoid the kit variety, as they tend to contain cheap fabric and flimsy frames. A better bet might be shopping for one at a supply house for the screenprint industry, which can be found in larger cities. These merchants offer beautifully stretched screens with wood or aluminum frames, usually at reasonable prices. These are also good places to buy squeegees, ink, photo emulsion, and stencil remover liquid.

TIP

Invest in a good squeegee bigger than your image and smaller than the frame of your screen. Get one with a wooden or aluminum handle and a thick, sharp blade, avoiding the skimpy rubber and plastic jobs that come in a kit. Transparencies can be made by hand or at a copy shop.

Coating the Screen

You can buy water-based photo emulsion by the pint, quart, or gallon. Speedball Diazo Photo Screen Printing Emulsion and Ulano TZ are good options. Follow the directions on the package. Water-based photo emulsions typically come in two parts: a container of goo and a bottle of sensitizer. The sensitizer makes the goo react to light. If the sensitizer is a powder, add water to it, shake it up, and add it to the emulsion. Stir the mixture with a long-blade spatula or a paint-stirring stick. Do this in a darkened room (because the emulsion is not super-reactive, the room does not have to be completely dark). Red or yellow light bulbs can help you see in the dark and not prematurely expose the sensitized emulsion.

Coat the screen with the emulsion using a squeegee. Buy a squeegee that fits inside the frame of your screen. Professionals use a specialty aluminum coating trough. Prop the screen upright against the wall at an angle. Pour a ribbon of the sensitized emulsion across the blade of your squeegee. Press the squeegee against the screen at the bottom, push forward firmly with two hands, and tilt the squeegee up, letting the goo flow until it makes contact with the whole width of the screen. Now scrape upward with the squeegee, pressing firmly against the screen the whole time, depositing a thin, even coat of emulsion across the entire screen, bottom

When coating the screen with photo emulsion, you can get by with a squeegee, but a coating trough like that seen here is custom made for the job. In a dim room, pour sensitized emulsion into the trough, hold it against the screen, and tilt it forward until a bead of goo touches the screen all the way across. Then pull up, pushing against the fabric the entire time. Don't yank the trough away when you get to the top. Instead, tilt it back and let the emulsion flow back in. *Demonstrated by Craig Upright*

to top. Once near the top, don't pull back abruptly, or runny strings will drip down the screen. Instead, keep pressing the squeegee against the screen, tilt it back and downward, and scrape up the last few inches in that position, and the last of the emulsion will flow nicely back onto the squeegee blade, avoiding drips. Wash your hands, spatula, and squeegee when done. Although it's technically nontoxic, don't ingest the stuff.

Let the screen dry in a darkened room. You can speed up drying time by placing a fan in front of the screen, but make sure to get any dust or debris out of the way of the wet screen. Don't expose the screen until it is dry to the touch on both sides.

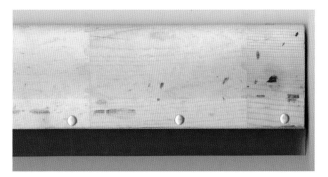

Invest in a good squeegee with a wooden handle and a thick, sharp blade. Avoid the skimpy, rubber and plastic jobs that come in kits. The blade should have some give but not collapse under your hands as you pull.

Exposure

A primitive but very effective exposure unit can be made with a quartz shop light purchased from a hardware or home store. The quartz light provides the proper color temperature to expose the photo emulsion. Also get a clean piece of glass, bigger than your transparency but small enough to fit inside the screen frame.

Suspend the quartz light 30 inches above the floor or table and plug it into an electrical outlet.

You can make an exposure rig using a quartz light and a piece of glass. Dangle the light 30 inches above your coated screen in a darkened room. This 500-watt construction-site light from Utilitech is an example of such a light. The halogen bulb is extremely bright with a color temperature that mimics daylight.

Lay the dry, coated screen, squeegee side up, horizontally on the floor or table. Place your transparency face up or "right reading" on the squeegee side of the screen. Use the clean piece of glass to hold down the positive and to ensure good contact between the emulsion and the image.

Now expose the coated screen by turning on the light for the manufacturer's suggested length of time. Seven and a half minutes is normal. Areas that are exposed to light will harden. Areas of the emulsion protected from light by dark parts of the transparency will stay soft.

Washout

Rinse the screen with **warm** (not hot!) water. The soft areas of the emulsion will wash out, leaving only the hardened emulsion in the screen. When printing, the hardened emulsion will hold ink back from the material

This red darkroom light made from a rotating emergency vehicle flasher is used by the Living Proof Collective. Red lights aren't necessary, as screenprint photo emulsion isn't overly sensitive to light. However, a red light will cut down on unnecessary exposure so your unused emulsion will last longer.

TIP

Areas that don't rinse out easily indicate the exposure was too long (overexposed). Wash out the stencil, dry, and recoat the screen. Reexpose using one-half minute less time. Images that rinse out too easily and don't hold in the screen indicate the exposure was too short (underexposed). Wash out the stencil, dry, and recoat the screen. Reexpose using one-half minute more time.

Washout after exposure. Rinse in **warm** (not hot) water until the softened emulsion falls away. Held up to a light, it will be evident where the ink can pass through the screen. Rinsing can be done in daylight. Stop rinsing once the last of the soft emulsion is out and place the screen in front of a fan to dry. *Demonstrated by Larsen Husby*

to be printed. The exposed areas of the screen formerly covered with soft emulsion will allow ink to pass through the surface to be printed.

A small screen can be washed out in a kitchen or utility sink. A dish sprayer can help focus the spray on areas of soft emulsion. A bathroom shower head can also work. If you use a high-pressure hose, be careful not to blast out the stencil.

Air or fan dry.

Printing

Now it's time to prepare the work area and tools for printing. This is called "make ready."

First, duct tape gutters or barricades between the frame and the screen on the squeegee side of your screen. This keeps ink from seeping into the gaps and inconveniently leaking out while printing. Also at this time, block off with newsprint any parts of the stencil or screen that shouldn't be printed on the bottom side of your screen. Tape the newsprint to the edges of the screen frame—don't use tape itself for the blockout. Newsprint works better than tape here. Just as Band-Aids fall off in the shower, masking

tape doesn't stick well with water-based inks, while duct tape is too bulky and can make the squeegee ride up, so use it in the gutters only.

Registration

Here's where a printing rig comes in handy. This is simply a board or table with hinges attached, which in turn attach to the screen to hold it in place. Fix the screen in the printing rig and tighten the hinge clamps. This ensures that each printed image is placed on the paper in the same spot each time. It also permits the printer to register, or line up, each consecutive printed image when executing multiple-color prints.

Tape the gutters and inner corners of the screen with duct tape before printing. Ink likes to leak under and in between the frame and the fabric and sneak out onto a print at the most inconvenient times. Making a tape gutter helps prevent leakage. Because the ink is water-based, use a waterproof tape. Masking or clear plastic tapes tend to fall off like Band-Aids in the shower.

Mask off borders on the bottom (print) side of the screen with masking tape and newsprint. Newsprint sticks surprisingly well to water-based ink, forming an effective barrier.

Line up where the paper should lie on the rig, in relation to the stencil in the screen. You can see through the screen before you lay down any ink. Holding the aligned paper in place, make some masking tape registration marks on the bottom board of the printing rig. One corner and one side are sufficient. These will remind you where to put the paper each time you print.

Alternately, register prints individually as you go with the use of a large sheet of clear acetate or Mylar plastic. Hinge the plastic to the edge of the table or screenprinting rig base very securely with tape. Lay it down on the table under the screen and pull the very first proof directly onto the plastic. Lift up the screen, pull back the plastic, and lay the printing paper on the table. Now flip the plastic back over the paper to see where to align the paper in relation to the print. Gently fold the plastic back on its hinge so it's out of the way, being careful not to

A printing rig consists of a board or table with hinge clamps that hold the screen in place while printing. It is indispensable for printing in multiple colors. The board stays put so the paper goes in the same place each time. Buy hinge clamps at screenprint supply houses. E-Z and Jiffy are two clamp brands. Door hinges have been used in a pinch, but the barrel cylinders prevent laying the screen flat, so they're not a great solution.

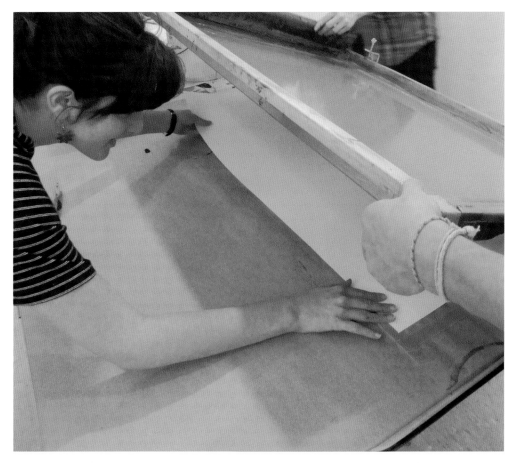

Simple masking tape registration involves marking a corner and a side to ensure you place the paper in the same spot every time. Build up a few layers of tape to make a bumper or backstop to help you place the paper quickly each time. *Demonstrated by Julia Sillen*

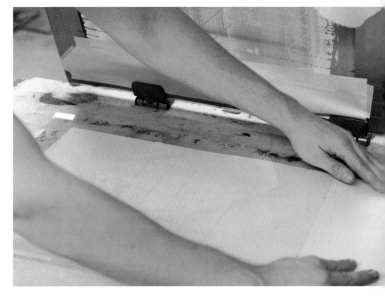

Here's another way to ensure registration. Print the first proof on a large sheet of plastic hinged to the table with tape, then flip it out of the way and lay down the printing paper. The advantage to the hinged plastic sheet system is that the wet ink flips out away from the printer.

Next, flip the printed plastic sheet back up over the paper to check registration. For critical close tolerance and fine registration, this action should be done with each print. It's also useful if printing on different sizes and shapes of paper, or if all the paper wasn't cut to the same size from the start. *Demonstrated by Larsen Husby*

Pour down a generous bead of ink as wide as the image near the stencil opening. Don't pour ink over any of the openings. Instead, the bead should sit in the gutter or on the margin in front of the image. This prevents seepage.

disturb the paper. Gently place the screen down and pull the squeegee. Repeat this process for every print. Mylar registration is also useful if the screen gets unhinged, something is off with the initial registration, or if you're using different sizes and shapes of papers.

Pulling Proofs and Prints

First, prop the screen up, away from the paper to be printed, using a jar, brick, or stick.

Insert the paper into the registration marks.

Pour down a bead of ink near the stencil opening, as wide as the image. To start, do not spread the ink over the opening(s) of the stencil. Screenprint inks can be acrylic or water-based. Water-based ink is not permanent, but it won't stain the screen, so it's good for beginners. Permanent acrylic ink must be printed very quickly, about every 10 seconds, or it dries and permanently clogs the screen fabric. Its advantage is that it can hold up on a poster outdoors in the rain. Inks of the same type can be mixed together to create unusual colors. Both will wash out of the screen with **cold** water after printing.

Lay the screen down on top of the paper to be printed.

Scrape ink across openings in the stencil in one quick, even motion, holding the squeegee at a low angle and pressing firmly. Squeegee well past the openings, coming to rest in the margins of the screen.

Now lift the screen and prop it up, and remove the print from the rig. Place it somewhere clean to dry or hang it from a clothesline. Professionals use a spring-loaded wire drying rack. Whatever you use, don't stack wet prints on top of each other!

Scrape ink across openings in the stencil in one quick, even motion, holding the squeegee at a low angle and pressing firmly. Feel for the table under the print. Don't lift up the squeegee until the image openings have been cleared. A backward "flood stroke" keeps wet ink in the openings. Do this with the screen up and off the paper. Gather a generous bead of ink the width of the image and scrape back over the openings. An incomplete flood will show up on the next print, so fill all the openings in the stencil. *Demonstrated by Larsen Husby*

Acrylic screenprinting ink must be printed very quickly, about every 10 seconds, or it dries and permanently clogs the screen fabric. Its advantage is that it can hold up outdoors in the rain. *Courtesy Speedball Art Products®*

A clothesline keeps wet prints from sticking together while drying. Clip prints back to back to save space. *Demonstrated by Drew Mintz and Julia Sillen*

Use cold water to rinse all ink out of both sides of the screen. This system lets you clean the screen while preserving the stencil, which only comes out in hot water. Rinsing ink out promptly means it won't clog in the screen. If ink sticks, gently use a scrub brush. Designate a separate scrub brush for ink only and never mix it up with one used for stencil remover liquids. *Demonstrated by Larsen Husby*

TIP
Use a proper-size squeegee, one that's bigger than the image but that fits comfortably inside the screen frame. Don't use a squeegee that's so large it rides up on the duct tape gutters. This can make for fuzzy details and leaking ink.

At this point, a backward "flood stroke" on the screen will keep the stencil juicy with ink while printing.

Repeat.

It's time to clean up. A large volume of ink is pushed back and forth across the screen during printing (be sure you have enough ink for the job before starting). Much of the ink can go back in the jar afterward for reuse. Undo the hinge clamps, remove any paper or masking tape from the screen, and take it to the washout sink. Use **cold** water and, if possible, a high-pressure hose to rinse all ink out of the screen. Rinse the squeegee, the spatula, and your hands as well.

Troubleshooting

Bleeding occurs when the printed images squish outside the image boundaries. To remedy, try taping small pieces of mat board to the underside of the screen frame to make the image "kiss off" quickly. Lift the screen promptly after each squeegee stroke. Prolonged contact of screen with paper causes bleeding.

TIP
Recruit a "catcher," someone to keep their hands clean and fetch the prints to dry. Printing by yourself is really hard when you're a beginner.

More than one stencil can be placed in the same large screen. Print them at different times by blocking out one with newsprint while you print the other.

If your image is too light, "salty" (i.e., speckled), or shrinking, the ink may be drying in the screen. Try pulling each squeegee stroke more slowly, but don't leave too much time between each print. Try wiping the underside of the screen with a wet paper towel, and then pull numerous newsprint proofs very rapidly. The first proofs will look sloppy, then they will heal up and print normally.

Screenprinting in Multiple Colors

Split Fountain

More than one stencil can be placed in a large screen at the same time. Print them at different times by blocking out one with newsprint while you print the other.

To print them at the same time in more than one color, use two or even three beads of ink and a long squeegee (a.k.a. the split fountain technique).

Two adjacent openings in different colors can also be printed at the same time by using two small squeegees along with two separate beads of ink. This is a good technique for adding a few spots of color that aren't so close to each other that the inks smear together during the printing process.

Blends

A blend is a classic, if sometimes kitschy, print technique for making multiple colors with one stroke of a squeegee. It transitions color across a design, producing different shades of one color or indicating light to dark effects, such as shadows.

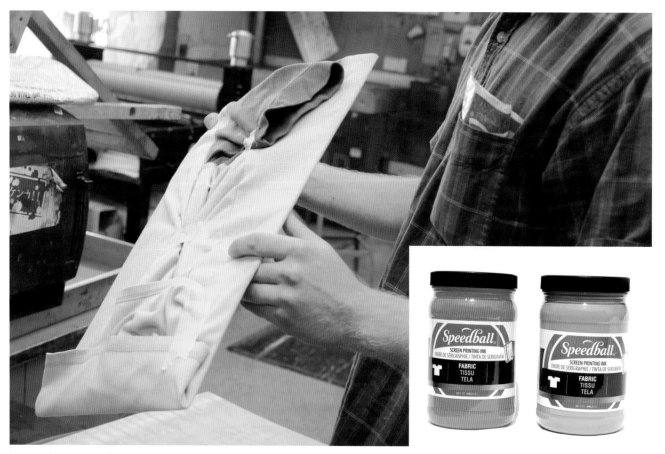

Use masking tape to bind shirt sleeves or excess fabric behind the cardboard. Left dangling, they tend to get inky. *Demonstrated by Zach Dotray* Inset: Manufacturers like Speedball offer inks formulated for screenprinting on fabric. *Courtesy Speedball Art Products®*

Place two beads of color next to each other sideways, along the same line. Leave a bit of space between the beads. Place the squeegee across both beads and wiggle slightly side to side, blending the two colors to make a third intermediate shade in the space between. Now pull the blend across the opening in the stencil. You should produce a color shift in the print image, from the first color, to a cross between the two colors, and over to the second color. Blends tend to mush together over a number of prints, so take care to place the squeegee down and scrape in the exact same position every time. Blending three or more colors is called a rainbow blend and takes extra skill.

Multiple Screens

With the above exceptions, multiple-color prints usually need a new screen for every new color. Wait for the first printed color to dry completely before printing another color. Previous prints can be taped to a window or laid on a light table to line up and cut a new stencil from paper, or to paint a new stencil on a clean screen. When using the photo-stencil method, new positive transparencies are created for each color to be printed. Access to a computer with Photoshop is useful for separating and lining up layers.

Printing a multiple-screen print requires precise registration, putting the paper down in the same place each time. Place the screen with the new stencil in the hinge clamps in the printing rig. Make a "marionette" by taping a yardstick to a good print from the first color run. This print-on-a-stick moves easily under the screen. Look through the stencil to align the first image with the next one to be printed. Put new tape marks on the bottom board of the rig along one corner and side of the puppet print and withdraw the marionette. All paper

Use a clothes iron to set the ink on printed fabric. Put paper over the inked surface so the iron stays clean. Heat-setting prevents the ink from coming out in the washing machine. *Demonstrated by Arella Vargas*

Howlers T-shirts stuffed with cardboard, printed, and placed on a wire drying rack.

will be placed in these new tape marks for this run. Remember, this only works if the first prints were all in the same place on the paper (that is, in register).

If you've ever wondered about those colorful marks on cereal box flaps, they're just another system of registration. Folding the box out flat, extra bits of cardboard are hidden off the main image area. Some printers leave wide borders on their paper and include a target mark on each stencil in that margin area. Lining up the crosshairs makes for accurate registration. The margins are trimmed down (or folded under the box top) after the colors are all printed.

Printing on T-Shirts

T-shirt printing follows most of the procedures above. A few extra planning steps will make the process go smoothly. First, be sure to wash shirts or any fabric before printing. Stores often coat textiles with silicone or starch, which interferes with ink. Stuff each shirt with smooth cardboard, such as foamboard or mat board, to create a flat surface for printing. Do not use corrugated brown cardboard as it produces stripes in the image. Don't use large cardboard that overstretches the shirts as this will result in a distorted image once the cardboard is taken

After soaking 20 minutes in liquid detergent, remove blockout stencils by spraying the screen with hot water. Don't skimp on the soaking time or permanent clogs could result. Use of a pressure washer is advised to really remove all traces of the stencil. Similarly, photo emulsion should be soaked in stencil remover liquid, then blasted with hot water. *Demonstrated by Mark Verdin*

TIP

Have a printing party with friends, fans, or bandmates. Offer free shirts in exchange for their help.

out. Use masking tape to bind sleeves or excess fabric behind the cardboard. Left dangling, they get inky. After the shirts are dry, heat-set the ink with a clothes iron. Put paper over the inked surface so the iron stays clean.

Reclaiming a Screen

Cleaning out an old stencil reclaims the screen to use for the next image or color. While paper stencils are simply peeled off, chemicals are needed to remove liquid blockout and photo emulsion.

Liquid blockout, such as Speedball Screen Filler, is dissolved with liquid detergents, such as Mr. Clean, while both Speedball and Ulano photo emulsions come out with Ulano Stencil Remover Liquid No. 4. Liquid bleach can also be used on photo emulsion, but it tends to be very smelly and caustic and so is not recommended, especially in unventilated areas. Stencil Remover Liquid No. 4 has no fumes and doesn't attack

your skin or your clothes. It can be found at screenprint suppliers and art stores.

The stencil removal process is the same in all cases. Lay down a large piece of plastic sheeting or a piece of Plexiglas and place the screen on top of it, squeegee side up. Pour about a half cup of soap or remover liquid over the screen and distribute with a scrub brush. Let the screen soak for at least 20 minutes. You will not necessarily see any stencil material dissolve. Then spray the screen with **hot** water, preferably using a high-pressure hose, starting in the center and working out. Home stores rent and sell portable pressure washers, which can be a great investment. Really blast the screen and remove any traces of stencil. Stencil left in the screen forms clogs that show up as skips in future prints, so be very thorough.

TIP

Take screens to be reclaimed to a self-service car wash. Soak screens in soap or stencil remover as needed atop a tarp or plastic sheet in the parking area. Use the high-pressure hose set on the hot-water rinse setting. Bring big trash bags for the wet clean screens and transport them home.

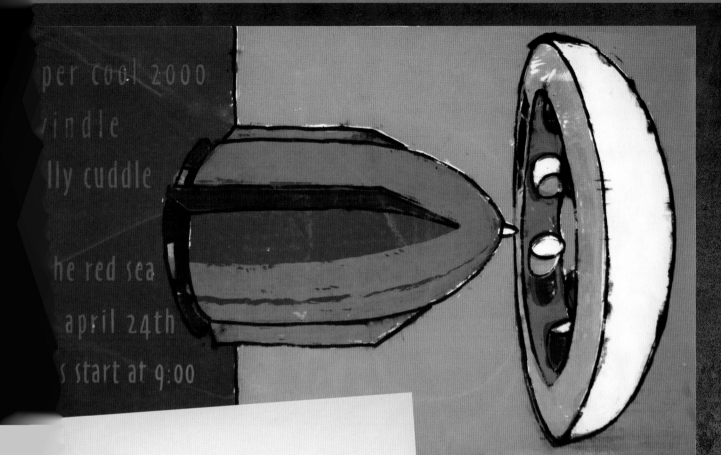

per cool 2000

indle

ly cuddle

he red sea

april 24th

start at 9:00

Above: Leaving a white space for a new color to go is called trapping. It creates a brighter effect than overprinting one color on top of another because the white of the paper reflects more light back to the eye, while overprints look a bit duller. Both effects are used in this screenprint poster for a multiband show. *Artist: Jeff Gillam*

Left: Newsprint paper, the same stuff the newspapers are printed on, tends to wrinkle under water-based ink and won't last long outdoors in the elements. It is, however, very affordable and holds detail well. *Artist: Jeff Gillam/ www.designrelated.com/drelatedjeffg*

dwindle.

COLFAX ABBEY

THE UPTOWN BAR

THURSDAY JAN. 25

101

SCREENPRINT IDEAS

Opposite: Early Dwindle screenprint poster by Jeff Gillam, whose work is featured in the book *The Art of Modern Rock*. www.designrelated. com/drelatedjeffg

Patches of various fabrics take ink quite differently. Screenprinting on a textile that already has a pattern can boost the impact of a one-color print, while fabric that is too dark tends to soak up colors and make them almost disappear. Fine weave muslin can print details as fine as paper can. *Artists: Mark Newman, Valerie Taylor, and Ginnie Hench*

More patches screenprinted on a variety of materials. Printing on heavy canvas can tend to lose fine detail, but the dark, thick denim seen here took pastel blue ink beautifully. Add white to any color to make a pastel tone, but start with white and add the stronger color (not the opposite). Just a touch of dark color in white or transparent base really alters the color dramatically.

Laying real objects on a scanner or photocopy glass can make for beautiful effects. Jeff Gillam used a small scissors and a locket on a chain, then fit the composition of the text around the forms.

Muerto Rider, a beautiful black-and-white relief print by Mexican artist Artemio Rodríguez. Rodríguez uses the Calavera motif—Day of the Dead skeletons engaged in and commenting on human activities in the tradition of José Guadelupe Posada, the famous Mexican print artist. *www.lamanografica.com*

Arella Vargas' poster for the Howlers is a simple and effective one-color print. Choosing a color paper background extends a one color print into two tones.

Paul Metzger's *Spontaneous Composition Generator* is a split 12-inch with Milo Fine's *Concerning the Other Condition*. Metzger's side of the sleeve features ghostly silver trees printed on a brown wrinkly paper reminiscent of 1950s pre-polypropylene sleeves. The cover was designed by Rich Barlow, and Metzger screenprinted the limited edition of 421 covers with Mandelbaum & Mandelbaum & Son. Milo Fine's side of the sleeve features the same design inverted. *www.neros-neptune.com and www.paulmetzger.net*

A mini screenprint from the prolific Jennifer Davis, printed at Burlesque of North America. Her distinctive line work and unique colors often result in odd animal themes, bicycles, and animal/human hybrids. *www.jenniferdavisart.com*

A screenprinted apron commemorating Motor Oil Industrial Coffee in St. Paul, Minnesota. *Artists: Motor Oil staff*

SCREENPRINT IDEAS

This screenprint poster to promote an Irrigate community event titled *We Are Here* was made at the Living Proof Collective. *Artist: Rose Holdorf/www. wehavelivingproof.com*

Two Tone Army. Ska groups of the '80s, including the long-lived band The Toasters, influenced punk music and helped break down color barriers. Adam Turman designed and screenprinted this scooter-riding beauty to commemorate the 30th anniversary tour of the iconic band, led by Bucket Hingley, who also founded Megalith Records. *www.adamturman.com* and *www.toasters.org*

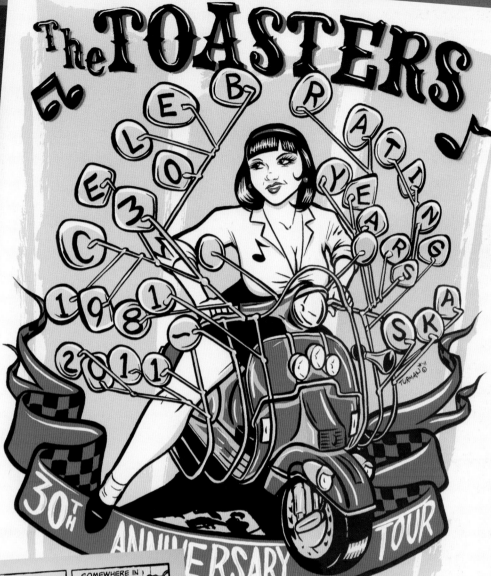

THE TOASTERS
CELEBRATING 30 YEARS SKA
1981 – 2011
30TH ANNIVERSARY TOUR

...ary 30 ★ SOMA ★ San Diego, CA
...ary 31 ★ Sidebar ★ Fullerton, CA
...ruary 1 ★ The Alley ★ Sparks, NV
...2 ★ The Blank Club ★ San Jose, CA
...Red Devil Lounge ★ San Francisco, CA
...4 ★ Red Fox Tavern ★ Eureka, CA
...ary 5 ★ Plan B ★ Portland, OR
...6 ★ The Venue ★ Vancouver, BC
...y 7 ★ Studio 7 ★ Seattle, WA
...ry 8 ★ A Club ★ Spokane, WA
...ry 9 ★ Shredder ★ Boise, ID
...rt's Tiki Lounge ★ Salt Lake City, UT
...wntown Grill & Venue ★ Casper, WY
...Black Sheep ★ Colorado Springs, CO

February 13 ★ Marquis Theatre ★ Denver, CO
February 14 ★ The Waiting Room ★ Omaha, NE
February 15 ★ Gabe's Oasis ★ Iowa City, IA
February 16 ★ Triple Rock Social Club ★ Minneapolis, MN
February 17 ★ Otto's ★ DeKalb, IL
February 18 ★ Firebird ★ Saint Louis, MO
February 19 ★ Melody Inn (Punk Rock Night) ★ Indianapolis, IN
February 20 ★ Frankie's ★ Toledo, OH
February 21 ★ Mac's Bar ★ Lansing, MI
February 22 ★ Musica ★ Akron, OH
February 23 ★ Mr. Smalls Theatre ★ Pittsburgh, PA
February 24 ★ Championship Bar & Grill ★ Trenton, NJ
February 25 ★ The Haunt ★ Ithaca, NY
February 26 ★ Club Hell ★ Providence, RI
February 27 ★ The Middle East ★ Cambridge, MA

...Toasters.org
...2011 AdamTurman.com

MEANWHILE...

...SOMEWHERE IN NORTH COUNTRY.

DEAD MAN WINTER

WITH RANDY WEEKS & JULIA KLATT SINGER
FEBRUARY 23, 2012
CEDAR CULTURAL CENTER
MINNEAPOLIS, MINNESOTA

Peet Fetsch uses a cartoon panel layout to create a narrative for the gig advertised in this screenprint poster. Ice-blue paper doubles as a wintry sky. *www.bigtablestudio.com*

This CD release poster makes spectacular use of just one color, bright yellow, and red paper. The image breaks out of the frame and moves the eye of the viewer to all the necessary information . . . *pow-pow-pow*. *Artist: Jeff Gillam*

Fruits & Veggies is a four-color screenprint by Burlesque of North America's Mike Davis. Pencil signatures and numbering are the traditional way of showing a fine-art print is approved by the artist and not a knockoff reprint. Prints produced in large quantities aren't generally pencil signed or numbered. *www.burlesquedesign.com*

The
BOMBAY
* RECORD RELEASE SHOW *
SWEETS

With

THE BLIND SHAKE
THE BIRTHDAY SUITS
BRUTE HEART
DJ JOHN REIS
SATURDAY, AUGUST 13, 2011
9PM • TURF CLUB

Aesthetic Apparatus duo Dan Ibarra and Michael Byzewski combine their mutual interest in printmaking and music to produce nationally recognized graphic designs, such as this screenprint poster for Bombay Sweets. *www.aestheticapparatus.com*

5

Stamping

A stamp just looks different than a crisp digital print. It has the feel of slight decay and implies bygone eras. Cylinder seals dating to 3500 BC in Mesopotamia were carved in stone and designed to leave an impression in wet clay or to print on cloth. Japanese anglers made records of their catch by inking fish and printing paper or cloth rubbings called gyotaku. Orville Wright and his childhood friend Ed Sines published a 'zine called *The Midget* on a toy rubber stamp press. And of course potatoes are still famous as cheap, carvable printing stamps.

The rubber stamp phenomenon is international. This nostalgic Japanese stamp is based on antique woodblock print imagery. Japanese-made papers, such as this green Moriki, take printed stamps beautifully.

The Fisher-Price Rubber Stamp Kit circa 1982 included directions printed inside the lid and an idea book. Yellow rubber upper- and lower-case letter shingles fit inside a 6-inch-long holder that allowed the user to keep a short line of text straight and aligned with the edge of a page.

THE BARE ESSENTIALS

- Stamp pads
- Rubber stamps (or items to be used as stamps)
- Paper
- Masking tape

Today, many vintage and retro images are available thanks to the rubber stamp revival seen at crafting stores in suburban malls. Secondhand stores also can be a source of rubber stamps, alphabets, and printing kits. Occasionally, interesting old advertising illustrations on wood and metal printing blocks from defunct letterpress operations show up in flea markets. These can all be inked up and used as stamps for interesting visual poster effects. Stamps can be inked to varying strengths for bold or pale, textured or distressed images as needed. Stamps are also great source material to incorporate into scanned digital images to create a more handmade and less mechanical look. Don't forget that one appealing aspect of stamping is that it requires no electricity!

Finding or Making Rubber Stamps

Finding rubber stamps is fairly simple, with whole stores devoted to the art of stamping and scrapbooking. Big selections of retro images are sold at craft, hobby, and art stores, as well as online. Secondhand stores pile them up in miscellaneous used office supply bins. Extremely useful sets of rubber type letters can still be found new, but check to make sure the whole alphabet is present if it's a secondhand set. Toy sets of letters and images, such as the 1980s Fisher-Price Printer's Kit, the dime-store junior printing set of the 1960s, and the Superior Ace Rotary Printing Press, still look and work great and can be found online and at yard sales and flea markets. Art supply stores will certainly have stamp pads, sometimes in the kiddie section. Office supply stores are yet another source of stamp pads and ink to replenish them.

For a price, you can custom-order rubber stamps with your own design. Online services abound, or you can find crusty old local shops still cranking them out. The online process will require that you email a high-quality (i.e., high-contrast and high-

This Doomdrips logo with lightning zorches is a custom-made rubber stamp used on packaging and the back of Aesthetic Apparatus posters.
Artist: Michael Byzewski/www.doomdrips.com

Most vegetables and fruits have an interesting shape and pattern when cut in half and printed. Paint some gouache or tempera poster paint over the surface and use your fruit half as a stamp. This design for a band called Eve 8 appropriately combined an apple and rubber stamps. *Artist: Rita Nadir*

Many found objects can be inked up and used as interesting stamps. Artist Chris Baumler cut out the shape of a bird, inked it, and printed it on cloth along with sumac leaves for the Kinship of Rivers flag-making project (www.kinshipofrivers.org).

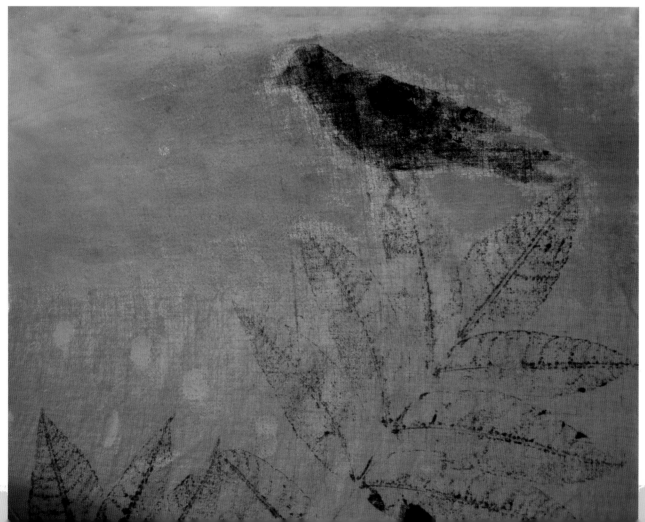

RUTHANN GODOLLEI

The Blind Lizard Rally is an annual vintage motorcycle and bicycle event in Minneapolis. Mailings feature the club house's return address as a premade rubber stamp and a lizard logo, which was probably a found item. *Courtesy Paul McLeete*

resolution, such as 600 ppi minimum) black-and-white digital graphic in the exact size the stamp is going to print. Many sites don't accept jpegs, so use a computer program such as Photoshop, Illustrator, or InDesign to make a TIFF file or a vector graphic. Follow the online specifications and upload instructions. There are self-inking varieties of stamps, but a stamp pad allows for more variation as you print.

Most vegetables and fruits cut in half have an interesting shape and pattern when printed. Potatoes have a uniformly dense texture and an even surface, so they can be halved, carved down about 1/4 inch, and the resulting relief surface used as a stamp.

Besides a potato half, you can carve your own stamps out of soft plastic or rubber erasers. Art stores sell oversize blocks of eraser material for this purpose. Use specialty gouges or carve with a small utility knife. Carved linoleum can also be used as a stamp, but softer plastic or rubber material generally stamps better. Images that are carved below the surface will "skip," while the remaining surface will ink up on the stamp pad and print. Remember to carve backward so the image prints forward.

Many found objects can be inked up and used as interesting stamps. If you think about it, the bottom of sneakers leave impressions in the sand, mud, and snow. Custom imprint flip-flops and sneakers inhabit a niche advertising market. Sponges have an interesting open-cell organic texture when printed. Foam toys and letters

Rubber stamps can be inked to varying strengths for bold or pale, textured or distressed images as needed.

A collage of rubber-stamp images illustrates varied ink strengths and printing in multiple colors.

TIP

Some stamps, especially those with used, worn surfaces, print better on a stack of papers than against one sheet on a hard table. Stack up little bits of paper "packing" under the printing paper. They will compensate for any divots, dents, or defects in the stamp. Rocking the stamp a little side to side deposits more of the ink.

Two pieces of material and an item inked back and front can make two prints at once. First, select an item to be inked. Here the poet Wang Ping uses a native grass during a Kinship of Rivers (www.kinshipofrivers.org) public flag-making workshop. Flags honoring the Mississippi River are made to be traded with folks from communities along the Yangtze River in China. Both rivers face similar environmental, cultural, and economic challenges. *Demonstrated by Wang Ping*

The item to be printed is laid in the ink slab and rolled with an inky brayer. The rolling pressure from above inks both the top and bottom of the grass. Inked on both sides, the grass is carefully placed on the bottom piece of fabric.

A second piece of cloth is placed over the bottom piece of fabric and the inked-up item to be printed.

116

Wang Ping rubs firmly, feeling for details of the inked material. The veins and stems of plants will print with outstanding detail if proper pressure is applied.

The inked item is removed and ready to be inked again. Here, two prints of a stalk of grass were made at once.

have similar cellular textures when used for printing. A big craze in DIY wall décor a few years back was stamped sponge painting meant to add texture that implied marble surfaces while it sneakily covered defects in the plaster. Wood and metal relief image and type blocks can all be hand stamped instead of letterpress printed. Vintage wooden toy blocks with individual letters carved on each make for great stamps with the bonus of a bit of wood grain. Leaves, gaskets, plastic and wooden toys, Styrofoam, cork, fish, tires, and anything relatively flat with a bit of texture can be inked and printed. Stamps can also be made from cutout pieces of cardboard, textured fabric, or heavy paper.

Inking

Stamp pads are designed to distribute ink reliably across the surface of a rubber stamp in an array of colors. As the stamping craft craze continues, inks are now available in pearl, metallic, and cracked or distressed tones. Pads are usually inside a hinged flat tin designed to keep the ink from drying out. They are typically foam sponges or cloth-covered felt. Office supply stores stock refill bottles with handy roller tops for reviving dried-out pads. Press the stamp or item to be inked face down in the pad with a gentle side-to-side rocking motion to ink it up.

Carved potatoes and other vegetables can be pressed in a stamp pad. They can also be brush-painted with watercolor, poster paint, or a thickened water-based paint called gouache, but painted blocks will generally produce a smeary, smudged look. Crafting sites offer specialized paints, such as those designed to crack and peel for a distressed, weathered effect.

Another way of inking a stamp, which is particularly helpful with found objects, is to roll out a slab of printing ink on a plastic plate or a dining hall tray as in the rollup stencil process (see Chapter 1). Ink up the object to be stamped, then proceed to print with it. This is a good method for printing fabric patches, bandanas, and T-shirts. Since stamp pad ink is less densely pigmented than relief ink, it doesn't tend to show up well or last on textiles. Stuff T-shirts with cardboard ahead of time so the stamps have something to press against. Be aware that if you ink up objects with oil-based ink, they might be permanently stained.

TIP

One trick for making a hand-printed paper sticker able to withstand the elements is to let it dry thoroughly and then coat it with a sealant, such as hairspray or clear coat spray paint. Krylon makes a clear acrylic spray coating that comes in glass and matte finishes. It's UV resistant so prints won't fade as much in strong sunlight. Use ventilation when applying.

Printing

After inking your stamp, press it face down onto paper. This process, while simple, allows for subtle variations. Notice if you press a fully inked stamp you get a "full strength" image on the paper, but if you don't re-ink the stamp before reprinting, you get a paler or "ghost" version of the image. Have fun varying the strength of the ink and placement of the repetitions. You can also ink the stamps in multiple colors if you have more than one color pad.

Stamp pad ink can be water-, alcohol-, or oil-based, and it tends to print better on somewhat absorbent, softer paper. Copy paper is fine, but ink tends to smear on coated or sealed papers and plastics. Japanese papers, such as Mulberry paper and the so-called rice papers, take stamp pad ink well. They can be found in art stores. Make sure the prints are dry before stacking.

Sticker paper can be printed, but get the kind that isn't too shiny unless you have the specialty ink for plastics. One trick for making a hand-printed paper sticker able to withstand the elements is to let it dry and then coat it with a sealant, such as hairspray or clear coat spray paint.

One advantage the lowly rubber stamp offers over letterpress printing is the ability to place the image spontaneously, in any orientation, on the page. Stamped images have the freedom to go where no press-bound letters can go.

If you ink up a flat object, such as a leaf or paper cutout, on both sides using the rollup method, you can either fold paper or fabric around and over it or use two pieces of material and get two prints at once. Roll out a slab of ink. Lay the object to be double-printed on top of the slab. Continue rolling ink on top of the object. The pressure of your rolling action will press the bottom of the object into the ink on the slab while the top is also getting inked. Lay the material to be printed onto the table. Place the object, now inked on both sides, onto the material. Place a second sheet of cloth or paper over both the bottom cloth and the inked item. Rub the back of the top cloth or paper firmly. Lift up and remove the inked object. You have simultaneously made a back and front impression of that object, that is, two prints at once. Alternatively, fold the material over the inked object, rub through the top (back) of the sheet, unfold, and find two prints on the same page.

The Red Seal Tradition

Red seals found on prints and artwork from China, Japan, and Korea are usually signature seals of the artists, studios, collectors of the work, and government censors. Collectors carefully consider where to place a seal on a work of art to add to its aesthetics and not detract from it. In China, seals are often carved from soft stone but can be made of wood or ivory and are inked via stamp pads with a distinctive crimson ink or a thick paste made of cinnabar, silk strands, and castor oil. Emperors used elaborately carved jade seals. Many people today still have stone seals made of their name that they use to sign formal documents. Tourists can get loose translations of their names in stone-carved seals or rubber stamps online or in Asian markets. Consider making your own seal and using it on all your products.

Cleanup

Press stamps onto clean paper without re-inking until most of the ink is gone from the surface. Usually that is all the cleaning required. Solvents are not recommended for cleaning real rubber as they will dissolve the surface. Be sure to close the cover of the stamp pad so the ink doesn't dry out. Wash your hands and any table surfaces that you inadvertently stamped.

If you used the rollup method, follow cleanup directions found in Chapter 1.

Rubber stamp with my name spelled phonetically in Japanese. Anyone can get a loose translation of their name in stone-carved seals or rubber stamps online or in Asian markets.

A blank green stone Chinese signature seal prior to carving. The handle of a stone seal can be simple or elaborately carved. *Courtesy Ray Hayward/tctaichi.org*

This detail of an 1852 Japanese woodcut print by Ichiyûsai Kuniyoshi shows an array of stamped seals, including the artist's signature, Kuniyoshi *ga* (made by Kuniyoshi), in a red gourd-shaped cartouche; the round seals of the censors Fuku & Muramatsu; and an oval date seal. Note the square red Yoshi Kiri seal (pawlownia flower) used by the artist. The scene shows the actor Bandô Shuka I as temple shirabyôshi dancer Hanako. *Author collection*

Closeup of a 1930s woodblock postcard print, *Zojoji Temple in Snow*, by Japanese artist Tsuchiya Koitsu. Signatures of both the artist and the publisher, Shôbidô Tanaka, show in red and black seals. Many people in Asia still have seals made of their name, which they use to sign formal documents. *Author collection*

A piece of masking tape, as its name implies, will temporarily mask out portions of a rubber stamp to prevent that part from printing. Ink the stamp, cover with tape, then print. The masked-out part can then be filled in with another image. Here, masking tape was used to block out the flowers in the basket of the bicycle in the rubber stamp. A red ball was then added, made to fall out of the basket and do a little twirl in a sequence reminiscent of animation.

Masking

Rubber stamps can be masked for interesting partial-printing effects. If you lay an intermediate piece of paper down on the surface to be printed, you can ink up a stamp and print some of the image on the surface and some on the paper that is blocking out part of it. Lift up the masking paper and observe that only part of the stamp has been printed. Alternatively, ink the stamp, cover a portion of it with a bit of masking tape, then print. The masked-out part skips. That area can be filled in with a contrasting color or a new image, collage-style.

So, for example, you could print half of a face peering over a wall or popping out of an egg. Or leave a hole in the center of a stamped flower by printing over a mask made out of a circle of paper cut that size. The hole could be filled in with a new image or overprinted with the same stamp, but in a different color.

Experimenting with masks allows the maker to radiate colors across an image, juxtapose images in surprising ways, or create sequences of visual events. Some wonderful stop-motion animations have been made with the humble printed stamp and masking techniques.

Stamping into Soft Surfaces

Some construction sites will post a guard to make sure no one is tempted to press their hands into, write their name on, or draw pictures in wet cement. If the cement is yours, however, no one is stopping you. Grauman's Chinese Theatre in Hollywood famously hosts the

The world's longest linoleum print was made in Kansas City, Missouri, in 2007. Members of Studio Rojo spent a month cutting the lino and then met up with guests and spread massive amounts of ink and unfurled a large roll of paper. Hundreds of participant printers each received a commemorative wooden spoon (used to rub the paper) rubber stamped for the occasion. The print, based on the children's story "The Five Brothers," was more than 3 feet tall and 90 feet long.

Poet Marcus Young teamed up with the St. Paul Public Works Department to imprint poetry in new sidewalk slabs. For the Everyday Poems for City Sidewalk project, an annual poetry contest is held, large plastic stamps are made, and city workers install open-air "books" for the public to enjoy as they walk.

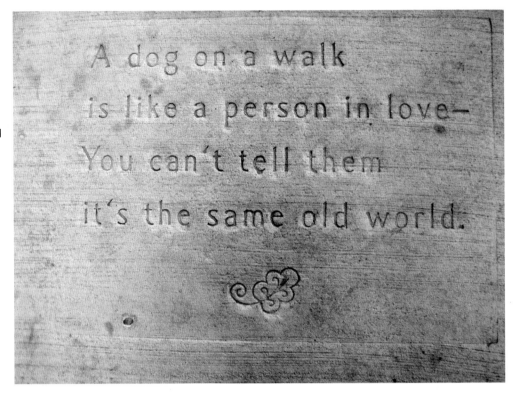

signatures, footprints, and handprints of film stars from the 1920s to today. Other objects, such as Harold Lloyd's glasses, the wands of the Harry Potter series' main actors, and Groucho Marx's cigar have been imprinted there. Plastic letters can also be pressed into wet cement, clay, or mud to make repeatable impressions. So can shoes, cookie cutters, tools, leaves, sticks, and carved wood or linoleum. Just remember to wash items off promptly so they aren't permanently caked with the material. Also keep in mind that images and letters must be backward to stamp forward, so you would need to use the back of plastic letters to have them read correctly when stamped. Dig out the small magnets from the backs of plastic refrigerator letter sets. You can also use wood or metal relief-printing type, which comes facing backward, but since many of these are precious antiques to printers, don't borrow them without permission. If cleaned promptly, they should be fine. However, don't soak wood type in water—rinse or daub with a damp sponge and dry quickly.

Poet Marcus Young teamed up with the St. Paul Public Works Department to imprint poetry in cement as broken sidewalks are replaced. For the Everyday Poems for City Sidewalk project, an annual poetry contest is held, large plastic stamps are made, and city cement workers install open air "books" for the public to enjoy as they walk. The stamps are fairly low relief, so the sidewalk's normal use is not affected.

Similarly, tiles of wet clay can be imprinted with your message or image, but in a portable manner. Clay centers and community arts programs offering ceramics teach the basics of tile-making and can fire them for you. Tiles, in turn, can make fine durable stamps for printing.

Historical Mobile Printing Devices

Many ingenious mobile printing devices have been produced over the years. In 1895 a French inventor introduced a printing tricycle. Solid rubber wheels were fitted with carved or cast printing blocks in designs that were automatically inked by gravity-fed rollers located under and behind the seat. The trike was meant to stamp prints on smooth paved roadways wherever the rider went pedaling.

Arya Pandjalu made Roda Roda Gila, a five-wheel bicycle printing unit that stencils *Pelan Pelan Aku Pasti*

PRINTING ON FOOD

Printing on food is possible with the use of edible inks. These beautiful tortillas were stamped in folk art motifs with a ceramic block at the Festival de Maguey, El Charco Ingenio nature preserve, San Miguel de Allende, Mexico.

This ceramic tile used as a food-stamping block is impervious to liquid and is washable. The tile's relief surface is daubed with edible blue juice, likely made from red cabbage and baking soda, and then pressed on tortillas before cooking.

Wood blocks "inked" with a corn cob soaked in red beet juice and used to stamp images into tortillas just before toasting on a hot griddle in San Miguel de Allende.

PUBLICITE PAR LA VÉLO
2ᵉ SALON DU CYCLE · PALAIS

Sampai (Slowly, I will arrive) through its perforated wheels in the streets of Yogyakarta, Indonesia.

Today, the Chalkbot is a trailer-mounted version of an oversize inkjet printer for chalk. It pneumatically sprays digitally created text or graphics onto pavement. DIY inventor Joshua Kinberg developed an earlier bicycle-mounted version designed for stenciling removable protest graphics on the streets.

Mexican artist Betsabee Romero carves used tires and prints the results, in addition to making large-scale installations with cars and their parts. Based on the thrifty make-do practices of the poor who sipe (regroove) their balding tires with gouges or hot wires to get a few more miles of use, Romero was inspired to remake tires into giant round rubber stamps. She inks up the tires in performances and gives free prints to people who hand her something to print on—paper, dishtowels, T-shirts, whatever. Displaying pre-Columbian imagery

In 1895 a French inventor introduced a printing tricycle. Solid rubber wheels were fitted with printing blocks bearing designs that were automatically inked by gravity-fed rollers under and behind the seat. The trike was meant to stamp prints on smooth, paved roadways wherever the rider went pedaling.

and patterns, her work also comments on disposable consumer culture.

Eric Fuertes uses his skills as a sculptor to collaborate with printers, making elaborate imaginative printing devices. He has made rocking horse printers, skateboard printers, and an interactive jump-on-the-bed press, operated by delighted participants invited to partake in that forbidden act of childhood. He has even cast halves of potatoes in bronze, had artists etch the flat surfaces, and then opened a combination French fry stand/mobile potato printing press. Patrons could order hot fries and fresh-off-the-press art during the Carnival of Ink at the Old Iron Works in New Orleans.

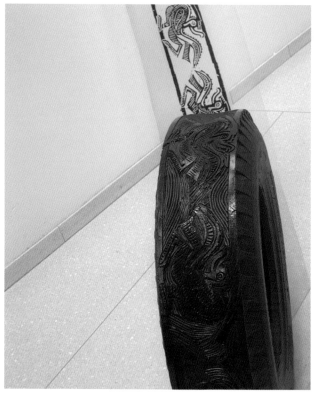

In performances artist Betsabee Romero inks up the tires she has carved in relief patterns and gives free prints to people who hand her items to print on.

Mexican artist Betsabee Romero carves used tires and prints the results. Observing the thrifty make-do practices of the poor who sipe (regroove) their balding tires with gouges and hot wires to get a few more miles out of them, Romero was inspired to remake tires into giant round rubber stamps. Designs are inspired by pre-Columbian motifs.

By reusing tires as rubber stamps, Betsabee Romero manages to take recycling to the level of an art form. Her work also comments on global disposable consumer culture—each year mountains of tires fill up landfills and ocean floors.

Eric Fuertes uses his skills as a sculptor to collaborate with printers in making outrageous printing devices. Here, he cast halves of potatoes in bronze, had artists etch the flat surfaces, then opened a combination French fry stand/mobile potato printing press. Patrons could order hot fries and fresh-off-the-press art during the Carnival of Ink in New Orleans. *Demonstrated by Will Sclater*

MOTOR OIL
INDUSTRIAL
COFFEES
SAINT PAUL, Mn

This vintage Motor Oil sweatshirt was screenprinted from a rubber stamp design. *Artist: Craig Upright*

A square paper hat made from a single sheet of newsprint is traditional headgear for newspaper printers. This one is decorated with a rubber stamp. *Artist: Kayla Nussbaum*

five
decades
of
paintings & prints

This exhibit flyer features rubber-stamp text that was scanned and reprinted lithographically. *Nash Gallery, University of Minnesota*

This rubber stamp marks a poster by Burlesque of North America. Burlesque has designed, illustrated, and printed albums, posters, stickers, T-shirts, and multicolor art prints for clients including Arcade Fire, Rhymesayers, Kid Robot, Atmosphere, Stones Throw Records, and many others. They also have an online store. *www.burlesquedesign.com*

A scene from the Japanese novel *The Tale of Genji*, illustrated in woodcut by Kunisada II (1864). This detail features the signature stamp, Kunisada hitsu ("from the brush of Kunisada"), with a red toshidama seal. This circular toshidama is a good-luck symbol, depicting a twist of cloth containing small gifts of money to be given to children at the new year, hence the four lumps in the ring. *Author collection*

STAMPING IDEAS

"Long River, Big River," reads the stone seal for the Kinship of Rivers Project (*www.kinshipofrivers.org*). KOR intends to link communities along the Yangtze River in China with those of the Mississippi through art, music, and education. Public flagmaking workshops are held and the artwork stamped with this seal. More than 1,000 flags have been made in the United States and will travel for exchange with people in China and Tibet, the home of the headwaters of the Yangtze.

...ne of the more than 1,000 Kinship of ...vers flags that have been made in the ...nited States. *Artist: Signe Peterson*

...ist Chris Baumler made this banner for the ...ship of Rivers project with a paper cutout ...mp of a bird, inked and stamped plants, and ...d lettering and touches of painting. Banners ...e hung along the Mississippi River for a ...mer solstice music and dance concert.

WATER SUPPORTS LIFE

The cover art for *The Replacements Stink*, the infamous 1982 EP by the band The Replacements, originally featured a hand-thwacked rubber stamp imprint on a plain white sleeve. The first few thousand EPs were labor intensive, with band members and friends hand printing sleeves in black, red, and (in one case) black with a fake bar code made from a hand-carved potato. Reissues featured the scanned original stamp and centered the design tastefully askew. Today, the hand-printed sleeves are prized by collectors. *Brien Lilja collection*

from San Francisco, Lookout! recording artists

GREENDAY

with

TRINITY OF SWINE

ALL AGES

$4 ■ 7:30 PM

MONDAY AUGUST 5

SPEEDBOAT GALLERY / MOTOR OIL COFFEE
SELBY AVE ST PAUL

This pre-superstar Green Day poster was designed by Motor Oil staff in rubber stamp with re-photocopying used to convey the punk sound ethos in a simple black and white poster, circa 1992. Everybody's gotta start somewhere. *Courtesy Craig Upright/Motor Oil*

CHAPTER SIX

Now That You Have the Printing Bug ....

Many first-time poster and shirt printers enjoy the process so much that they want to do it again, perhaps knowing that the next time they'd do it a bit differently and better. But to keep going, you need access to equipment and materials, a workspace, and occasional advice.

This array of work by the Living Proof Print collective includes everything from an Occupy protest poster to a valentine. www.wehavelivingproof.com

Gathering Tools of the Trade

Equipment and materials can be found online, but paying shipping for an item you haven't seen in person or tried out yet is a bad idea. Going local when possible lets you talk to real people who know the products or can put you in contact with someone who does. Art supply store personnel have often demoed the equipment and materials, and some moonlight as printers themselves.

Screenprint supply houses know the professionals who use their equipment, and they often have business cards and samples of print work posted onsite, so track them down and visit their print shops.

Your local college or university might have equipment that you can access. If you know someone enrolled in the printmaking class, they may be able to do a collaborative project as an independent study. Or you may be able to volunteer your services to clean up, organize tools, build shelving, paint, clean out silkscreen stencils, or do any of the myriad chores any print shop always needs done, in exchange for access. At my college we have a long history of successful barters and trades along these lines, and consider it a form of community outreach.

Finally, art centers and community education programs offer print instruction for reasonable fees, and the growing EXCO (Experimental College) movement is an exciting free-education initiative available in some communities.

Printing these group project postcards "six up" saved paper, time, and labor. Limiting the colors was a design challenge, but also made the project easier to execute. Thicker cardstock paper was used so the prints could be sent through the mail. *Artists: Julia Sillen, Drew Mintz, Cove Fylpaa, Riley Hare, and Caroline Devany; courtesy the Irrigate Community Postcard Project/ www.irrigatearts.org*

Here's the run, stacked and ready for distribution. Satisfying, indeed. The backs were printed first, in black, with identifying information and lines for addressing the cards. *Courtesy the Irrigate Community Postcard Project/ www.irrigatearts.org*

Create a Workspace

Printing can take up a lot of space. If you organize your tasks and clean up after yourself, you can get by with a dining room table operation as long as you're not producing arena-size posters. Try to keep a clean table area, separate from where coating and cleanup processes will take place. Having a dedicated space where some equipment can be left out is ideal.

A utility sink for cleanup is the second priority after a large, flat tabletop. Get some good mechanic's pumice soap for inky hands and shop aprons or big old overclothes to keep ink off the wrong shirts. Rubber or plastic gloves protect skin during cleanup, but also keep hands, and thus prints, from getting inky while printing. Screenprinters should equip the sink with two scrub brushes: one for ink and one for emulsion-remover liquid.

The biggest space guzzler will be the prints themselves as they dry. Don't stack wet prints or they will stick to each other. One space-conserving way to dry a big run of prints is to hang clothesline and use good wooden or plastic clothespins (those with metal springs) or metal

Cutting a stack of prints with scissors or a utility knife gets old fast. A paper cutter with a sharp blade is a good investment. Avoid the newer plastic models if possible. Sturdy old heavy metal and wood cutters can be found used, but check to see that the blade is free of nicks, which can produce ragged cuts. Look for blade-sharpening services in larger cities. Tape marks placed on the bed guide where to place paper. *Demonstrated by Cove Fylpaa*

clips, or even large paperclips in a pinch, to keep the wet prints separate and the ink from getting all over everything. This method works well for T-shirts, too, of course (after all, it is a clothesline). Those more serious about printing might invest in a wire print-drying rack like the pros use. Keeping an electric fan running will help dry screenprint emulsion, but be careful as it can blow wet prints into one big stuck mess fast. If you use a fan, also be sure your area is relatively dust-free. You don't want tiny particles to become parts of your works of art.

Since prints are artworks made in multiple, even dry prints stack up fast. You hope to be able to give away or sell a lot of what you make, but you will need somewhere to store the inventory until that happens, and it's a good idea not to get pet hair, dust, or spilled beer on the merchandise. It is also a good idea to keep an archive of some sort, a record of the best things you made. Plastic tubs with lids work pretty well. Get the long, low ones made for storing shoes under the bed. Serious printers have flat files for keeping clean printing paper and finished prints in good condition. These shallow horizontal, metal or wooden drawers are purposefully designed to hold stacks of paper, such as blueprints in architectural firms or maps in libraries. These can sometimes be found at sales of used office equipment or at discount prices in office supply stores

when they have blemishes or dents. While you're at it, why not devote a wall as gallery space for showing off your finished work to admirers?

Cutting a big stack of prints with scissors or a utility knife by hand gets old fast, so a paper cutter with a good blade is another wish-list item. Used wood and steel cutters tend to be sturdier than the new plastic models available. Blades can be resharpened at a reasonable price if you look for local services.

A basic set of tools, including flathead and Phillips screwdrivers, a hammer, a saw, a utility knife, scissors, and a yardstick, are good survival tools for any human being. Metal yardsticks cost a fortune at art stores, but for some reason they are inexpensive at lumberyards and home stores. Wooden ones, less desirable because you might need to cut against them, are sometimes available free at fairs. A staple gun can be used to make screenprint screens and serves double duty when tacking posters to utility poles and plywood walls at construction sites. Heavy-duty extension cords of the three-pronged variety are safer and less prone to fire than cheap brown and white two-wire lamp cords. If you have the money, a variable speed drill with screwdriver bits, a power saw, a miter box, a jigsaw, and a power washer could all be on the shopping list.

A computer with graphics programs and a laser printer are very helpful, but several of the processes we've discussed don't require them. (If you acquire this sort of high-end equipment, think about securing your workspace.) Invest in a surge protector or buy one built into a multioutlet power strip and you won't have to worry about lightning frying all your hard work. Finally, how-to manuals and online tutorials are handy for the self-taught digital designer.

Good lighting is another key factor, as it will help you see proper registration and colors. Shelves and drawers, or perhaps a pegboard for ink and tools, will help keep small things organized. Forming or joining a print collective is a good option. Like being in a band, a group can pool resources, rent space, gather equipment, collate prints, and share chores as well as knowledge. Just having one extra person with clean hands when printing is a big help, but a group can build camaraderie and momentum. Sales of printed items can go back into the space and materials, so no one has to go broke.

Work with Professionals

As recommended earlier, visit professional print shops to see how it's done in the big leagues. Many printers hold open-house events or have a gallery attached to their shops. Some are generous with their time and advice. It doesn't hurt to strike up a conversation.

Use of a service bureau to make film transparencies, in addition to providing the highest-quality base images for photo processes, can also lead to useful connections and discussions of practices and practitioners.

Professional print shops are doing amazing work these days and are the best option for large quantities and complex graphics. Once you have a little experience under your belt, you will be better prepared to talk intelligently with pros about the look you want and how to get it. You also will have realistic ideas about the timeline and materials costs. At the very least you will have respect for the amount of labor and practice it takes to print well on demand and on deadline.

Your Local Art Supply Store

People often ask why I patronize my local art supply store when its prices are a bit higher on some items. First, mine happens to be in a convenient location, near my studio. Second, I can see the merchandise firsthand. I don't have to guess at the consistency of the materials, quality of the tools, or feel of the paper—the stuff is there for me to touch and compare. Third, the staffers, as in most art stores, are artists themselves and have actually tried the products. They are happy to talk to patrons about the differences between brands of products and able to discuss compatibility among materials and whether a high-end item is worth the cost. Free in-store demos are regular events and samples are on display throughout the store. Fourth, as a regular, I get the heads-up on sales of items I regularly buy and first dibs on slightly damaged goods and closeout items. Fifth, perhaps my local store is an exception, but it actually provides healthcare benefits to the workers. There are actually more reasons than I can count, but I do believe in buying local when possible. Some items really are only available online, and you might live in a small town or a remote area. Sadly, independent retailers of the brick and mortar

variety are on the decline, but my local art store will post flyers for my show in the window for free.

Service Bureaus for Film Transparencies and Oversize Prints

If you don't have your own copy machine or laser printer, the local copy center can suffice. Many of these shops are open late or even 24 hours a day. Either bring in a thumb drive or CD of your image file, or rent time on one of their computers to use the graphic software. You will save some money if the file is printer ready, sized to print at 100 percent scale for 8.5x11 or to the other standard paper sizes for oversize prints. Remember to include a border, as most photocopies don't print right to the edge of paper. Look up the print sizes available ahead of time so you know what your target output size should be. Stop by the copy shop for a brochure or look it up online. This background research will also prepare you for the costs entailed. Remember to get two transparencies if you are making a positive, and tape them together, so your transparency will be dense enough. Several transparency sheets can be taped together to make an oversize positive. The copy shop price for printing on plastic has a hefty margin built in, so if you do this a lot you can save money over time by investing in your own copier or printer and bulk boxes of transparencies.

Making positives with a copy machine or laser printer has its limitations. Many professionals take their work to a service bureau that makes real film transparencies. Only one is required, as these positives are dark, rich black, super sharp in detail, and available in sizes much larger than letter. They are not cheap, however. Look up the specifications online or, if it's a local business, stop by and get a price and services sheet. Here is your chance to ask a lot of good questions. Remember, a service bureau would like your returning business, so it should be willing to walk you through the format your file should be in, the amount of border needed, the size limitations of its equipment, the price structure, and the turnaround time. While you are there, find out what staffers there think is a good number of dots per inch for halftones for screenprints, or who in town does good poster work.

An assortment of business cards shows eye-catching graphics in tiny spaces. Usually featuring text and one image, the 2x3.5-inch layout can be a challenge. In some countries, like Japan, the tradition of exchanging business cards is taken seriously. The protocol involves holding the card in both hands and extending it to the receiver, who actually looks at it, puts it in a nice cardholder, and politely reciprocates.

Some service bureaus let you upload files online, but pick up the work in person. This is nearly ideal, as it saves one trip but puts you in contact with a real person when it counts. Be sure to open the envelope or tube and check the product before you leave the premises. If it's not right, you at least have the chance to have it fixed, sometimes quite promptly and without charge if it's their mistake. Here's where developing a relationship with a local business pays off. Some shops post examples of work done by their customers or let you leave business cards to advertise your abilities.

If a local service bureau is not available, you can upload files and have the transparencies mailed to you. Sometimes this is the only option, but mistakes can be a real headache. For beginning users of these sites, it isn't always clear, for example, how much border to leave, how to scale images properly, or what ppi to use in order to get good results with your particular printing

A collection of beautiful hand-printed business cards from professionals shows off the printers' art in miniature. Screenprints are from Big Table Studio and Burlesque of North America. Letterpress examples come from Lunalux, Independent Project Records, Bruno Press, and Yee-Haw Industries.

If business cards need to be made quickly, a computer and laser printer works well. Premade templates exist online, often available for download at websites listed on packages of handy preperforated cardstock available at office supply stores. Design cards for maximum visual impact and readability inside a small space. Set printer paper handling for heavy cardstock. *Courtesy Avery*

setup. If a mixup occurs, or you didn't follow directions perfectly, see if there is a live person available to talk to you on a helpline. Budget in the turnaround time. The U.S. Postal Service is still quite a bargain if you plan ahead. Many services will do expedited shipping, but for a hefty fee.

Oversize prints have been discussed in terms of stenciling in Chapter 1, but sometimes only one or two posters are needed, as for a marquee or promotion taped on the side of a van. Many copy shops can make these for you from a file, but be sure it is high enough resolution so the image doesn't lose detail when blown up that large. Higher-quality fine art prints are available at commensurate prices from digital graphic services. Somewhere in between the two, niche printing places doing small-run poster-size work can be affordable.

Business Cards

Leaving your business card with the professionals you work with is a good idea. Facebook may let your friends know when your show or event occurs, or how to reach you, but on the material plane it's a good idea to have something printed to hand to strangers. How else will someone remember your odd username or long website URL, or reach you by cellphone? The business card dates back to the nineteenth century when commercial printing became cheap and available to the average person. Previously, calling cards were the polite way wealthy people introduced themselves. The cards were handwritten in perfect penmanship and handed to servants at the door, carried about in elaborate dishes made of ceramics or silver, and formed part of the elaborate rituals of upper-class visitation. The contemporary business card should supply basic contact information but also provide an opportunity to tell people something about you through its aesthetics: images, design, text choices, originality, and style.

In some countries, like Japan, the tradition of exchanging business cards is taken quite seriously. The protocol involves holding the card in both hands and extending it to the receiver, who actually looks at it, puts it in a nice cardholder, and gives you theirs. Cardholders are not a bad idea, as your wallet will not hold very many cards, and they can get gross and sweaty in there. Gift stores and online retailers of stationery products sell them in a wide variety of styles, from industrial aluminum to pink rhinestone. The nicest ones come from Japan (no surprise there). Once you've gone to the bother of making original cards, keep them with you at all times. It is the most portable way to give someone a little souvenir.

You can certainly make your own business cards with any of the DIY printing processes detailed in earlier chapters. The look will be unique, therefore worth the time and labor involved. Select sturdy cardstock. Layout is often 10 up for the standard 8.5x11 piece of paper (with a $^1/_2$-inch margin included). It could be more or less on custom paper sizes. The paper itself can be a distinctive part of the design, just make sure it isn't so textured that the print doesn't read clearly.

If business cards need to be made quickly and easily, a computer and laser printer are your best bets. Premade

TIP

Don't let the design rest on any of the business card's borders. Leave at least 1/8 inch around each individual card. Commercial copiers and laser printers are simply not that accurate. Slight shifts in going through the machine can result in crucial texts, such as your email or phone number, misplaced outside the margins and/or images cut off or leaking onto the neighboring card. Also, design the card for maximum visual impact and readability inside a small space. Some fancy fonts are extra cool, but are unreadable in 9-point type. Ideally, the card should have a design so interesting people say "Wow" when it's handed to them, but most importantly, that makes it possible for someone to actually get in touch with you.

templates exist online and are available for download at websites listed in packages of handy preperforated cardstock available at office supply stores. Avery makes perfectly reliable, reasonably priced blank cards in 8.5x11 sheets. While limited in color choices, these sheets are designed to go through the printer or copy machine aligned exactly 10 up, with a $^1/_2$-inch margin all the way around, tearing apart easily into 2x3.5 cards once printed. Word programs or graphics software can be used to design the layouts.

Once the design for one 2x3.5 card is made, it can be grouped, selected, copied, and pasted nine more times and lined up inside the specified margins. It never hurts to print out a proof on cheap copy paper before committing to more expensive cardstock.

You can also order a set of business cards printed to your specifications online or from a local print shop. Cheap services will print rather mundane, if competent,

TIP

If there is room on your business card, list all the ways people can contact you—phone, e-mail, URL, Facebook, etc. Consider building in a QR code, the square block version of the barcode, which once scanned with a smartphone links the viewer to a website of your choice. If you are techno-savvy, have some fun with an interactive QR code project—no sense in boring viewers once you've made them jump through the hoops of scanning and downloading.

Printed novelty items, sometimes known as swag, can function as fun souvenirs or event promotions (and later, memorabilia). Cannonball Press uses combs and printed wooden coins to advertise their $20 bargain posters, while preprinted pencils, tin badges, stickers, and professionally embroidered patches can all be ordered on demand. McClain's Printmaking Supplies hands out temporary tattoos with the motto "Live to Print."

A jig is a holder for easily positioning an item while printing. Here, a hollow was made by carving out foamboard in order to letterpress print pencils. This device could also work for screenprinting. While pros use purpose-made gauge pins to hold letterpress paper and printable items in place in the press, a thumbtack with a flat head stuck in the foamboard could help hold the pencil in place in a pinch.

versions with a limited selection of clip art and fonts. I personally think it is worth the time and labor to create and print your own, or the investment to have someone else print for you something that won't give people the urge to toss your card into the nearest trash bin. Why not work with a hand-printed stationery shop, such as Lunalux (www.lunalux.com), which will custom print an embossed card on unique paper with its vintage letterpress equipment? The luxurious look is both antique and contemporary and will grab the viewer's attention.

Printed Objects

Novelty printed items, sometimes known as swag, can function as fun souvenirs or event promotions, and later as memorabilia. Printing on three-dimensional objects presents unique challenges. Usually the printer needs to make a specialty jig, or holder, so the item stays put

while one surface is printed. If you are going to print an unusual object, it is extremely helpful if it has one flat surface. Pencils, pens, toothbrushes, keychain fobs, mouse pads, coasters, beer cozies, hair combs, matchbook covers, and more can all be printed. Try your print technique on a sample first, checking that the image or text is readable and that the ink dries well and doesn't peel off. Then buy a case or cases of your blank objects so they're all the same size and shape. Many such items are cheaper purchased in bulk. With a little preparation, small three-dimensional objects can be hand printed efficiently and in fairly large quantities.

One way to screenprint or letterpress print on an object is to trace around the outside of the item on a piece of foamboard, and then use a utility knife or X-Acto blade to cut a snug-fitting nest or depression for the object to be printed. The printable surface should just barely peek out over the top of its holder. Tape this foamboard jig to

Business cards that are die cut, folded, or embossed present a more unique look than those printed on plain white paper. Art and craft stores stock machines for making your own simple cut shapes, while die-cutting services are available from some professional printers. The air freshener cards were spritzed with an extra confusing/amusing lemon scent.

a printing rig, adjust the pressure of the press or the height of the silkscreen by inserting some cardboard cards under the screen clamps or building up off contact height (see Chapter 4). This jig will let you insert a new pencil efficiently in the same spot every time, which is important, since small-size text and images tend to dry out, fill in, or clog up quickly. Should clogs occur, insert blank pieces of paper over the object and keep printing rapidly until the image is cleared.

If one were going to print on matchbook covers for a living, it would make sense to print on the cardstock first, cut it down, fold it, and finally staple it to the matches. Those of us without our own personal match factories get blank matchbooks by the case, unfold each, and make a little printing jig so it's easier to work with them. Again, creating a hollowed-out space in a piece of foamboard will make the process much easier, no matter which printing technique is used.

Printing tiny type and pictures on unusual surfaces is a fairly advanced skill, so it is no shame to hire professionals who do those tasks well. Services that make custom-imprinted objects charge less the more you order, often with an initial setup price. They can be found online under headings such as novelty items, corporate gifts, or promotional products.

Die Cutting

Die cutting refers to cookie-cutter-type blades called dies used to cut specialty shapes other than squares and rectangles in paper or cardstock. Die cutting is a branch of relief printing and can be done, with a bit of bother, on a letterpress. Thin pieces of sharpened metal or wire are fitted into cork or plastic bases and act as cutting blades. Pressure from the printing press cuts the paper to the shape formed by the blades. Heavy-duty backing material needs be placed behind the paper or cardstock to avoid slicing into the press or dulling the blades. Art and craft stores stock machines for making your own simple cut shapes, with varying quality of results. Ask to see a demo of one in action before committing to the purchase.

Round beverage coasters are probably the most familiar die-cut items. Art stores and online paper supply companies stock blank sheets of thick paper called pulp board or blotters used to print coasters. Cutting circles out of bricklike cardboard with hand scissors can quickly result in blisters. Precut blank coasters are real skin savers, and they can be printed with any of the do-it-yourself processes previously discussed. The purpose of a coaster is to absorb liquid, however, so runny water-based ink or stamp-pad prints may blur

a bit. Test your printing chops before committing to large quantities. Crafting supply places and online sites sell small quantities of blank coasters at high prices compared to bulk suppliers, which sometimes have minimum orders starting at 1,000. That is actually a large run for hand-printed work, so keep in mind your stamina and the patience of your friends and assistants.

Katz Americas ("more than just a beverage coaster"), a division of Kohler Paper Group, is an example of a bulk supplier of blank coasters, but they will also custom print slick picture coasters from an image file on demand and in full color, for a fee.

Other die-cut items, such as balsa wood glider planes, can be purchased blank and unassembled for self-printing, or custom imprinted to your specifications. The French Paper Company (www.frenchpaper.com) makes Decor-A-Boards, preprinted ready-to-hang wood art made of scalloped-edge birch veneer over MDF board and manufactured with recycled wood. Such items are just begging to be overprinted with custom graphics.

Buttons in varying sizes declare the wearers' sympathy with various causes, love of particular bands, and support for art projects. Over time they can become collectible souvenirs.

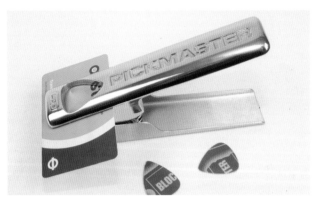

The Pickmaster plectrum cutter is a handheld die cutter for guitar picks. Currently sold only in Europe and the United Kingdom, its manufacturer suggests recycling unwanted plastic cards (such as gift cards), unsolicited corporate materials, or packaging into guitar picks on demand. The maker can have fun selecting graphics indicating the former life of the material. User reviews recommend filing off the rough edges of the freshly punched strumming tool on sandpaper, your jeans, or the sidewalk. *Courtesy Slam Design/ www.slamdesign.co.uk*

The Pickmaster plectrum punch (www.slamdesign. co.uk) is a handheld die cutter for guitar picks. Currently sold only in Europe and the United Kingdom, it allows the user to cut up used gift cards, unsolicited corporate material, and plastic packaging into guitar picks. The maker can have fun selecting graphics indicating the former life of the recycled material. User reviews recommend sanding off the rough edges of the freshly punched plectrum.

Buttons

Pinback buttons have become commonplace concert mementos, promotional items, and protest emblems. They can be ordered from numerous services online, made from your design, or bought in an array of predesigned products. If you like this form of wearable art, you might consider investing in a button-making machine. These typically come with a circle die cutter (or a device known as a graphic punch) and a supply of metal shells, pin backs, and clear plastic Mylar overlays, which get assembled in a sandwich and crimped together. You design and provide the printed or found artwork that fits inside the diameter of the button being made. Be sure to account for the slim wraparound space on the side of

TIP

It's a good idea to provide some identifying information somewhere on your button design. Some people put their URL in very tiny type in the side margin space, called the wraparound or the curl. This works best on larger buttons, as the crimped plastic on buttons smaller than 1 inch wide may interfere with curl image visibility.

the button, as it curves over the metal backing. Artwork should fit comfortably on the face of the button.

Artwork for buttons can be printed by hand or digitally and cut out by hand with scissors or with a die cutter or an adjustable rotary cutter. Round templates in the correct sizes are available in Photoshop Elements, or try free design software, such as Open Office (which has a draw feature). You will need to lay out the cut-line diameter of the circle and inside it the smaller face line, meaning the face of the button. You can always just trace around a quarter—it's the right size for 1-inch button artwork.

Directions for use of button-making devices vary between manufacturers. There are a lot of steps that need to be followed carefully, in order. Read through the directions before starting and keep them with you, following along step by step. Ideally work with another person, who can read the instructions to you and check the work as you go. In general, the device will come with a set of metal retaining rings, color-coded to aid in the process. The largest ring is usually laid face up. Pay attention to which way should face up (there are notches or markings on the ring to guide you). Next, the blank metal button front is laid face up in the ring, then the circular artwork and clear plastic cover. A retaining ring will go over all those layers and usually fits inside the largest ring. For many devices, the next procedure involves turning the assembly over and applying some pressure to get the layers snugly fitting together. This may also be the step where another ring or some form of cap starts crimping the plastic cover down over the artwork and button front. Next it is logical to turn the whole thing over and place the pin back on the back of the assembly. Make sure the pin is closed. In addition, make sure the orientation of the pin correlates with the

A rotary cutter, metal button blanks, pin backs, color-coded rings, and a hand press comprise the Badge-A-Minit button-making kit. Similar components will be found in other brands.

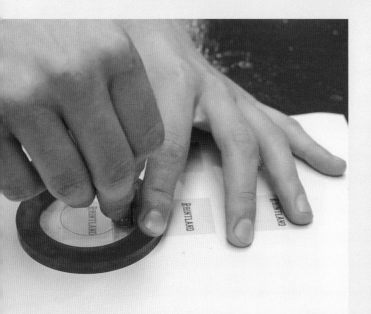

The rotary cutter tool is used here to cut out circular artwork properly sized for the button being made. A circular die cutter or a device known as a graphic punch both make perfect circles out of your artwork. Scissors work fine, too. First trace something circular. A quarter is about the right size for a 1-inch-diameter button. *Demonstrated by Christian Behrends*

You will also need circles of clear Mylar plastic to cover the buttons. Some kits include stacks of precut plastic circles; they can also be bought as extras. Be sure to lay a few sheets of paper underneath the material being cut. It not only keeps the tabletop from getting scratched up, but it also leads to smoother cuts with fewer snags and more perfect circles.

Lay a metal button blank face up in the largest ring, followed by a sandwich of artwork and the clear plastic cover. Next, a retaining ring and some kind of pressure cap are applied, initially crimping the plastic over and around the artwork and the button. Follow the instructions for your particular button maker closely—the order of the steps affects the outcome.

Next turn the whole thing over and place the pin back on the back of the assembly. Make sure the pin is closed and that the orientation of the pin correlates with the orientation of the image. You usually don't want viewers to have to turn their heads sideways to read your button.

With another retaining cap in place, a hand press is used to smush all the parts together, producing a finished button. Some kits feature a tabletop press, but the principle is the same. The pressure and the crimping seal all the components in place.

Artwork should fit comfortably on the face of the button.

orientation of the image. In other words, you don't want a pin running vertically up and down, which will make the image appear sideways when the button is pinned to your shirt. There should be notches, grooves, or other clues on the rings to aid in proper placement of the pin back, but use a little back-to-front thinking and check to see if the placement makes sense. Last, either a hand press or a tabletop press, the largest feature of a button-making kit, is used to smush all the parts together, producing a finished button. My advice is to be patient and, as with all learning processes, build in some extra materials and time and count on losing some of each.

Temporary Tattoos

A friend of mine once swore the two things she'd never do was get married or get a tattoo. To psych everyone out at her wedding, she covered herself head to toe in hilariously garish temporary tattoos of the flaming skull, stabbed heart, and bleeding eyeball variety, then donned a lacy white dress. She certainly made a memorable impression as they played "Here Comes the Bride." As tattoos have entered mainstream culture, temporary tattoos are now available as custom-printed promotional items, sometimes quite inexpensively. Order them online. Make sure you get FDA-approved inks so you don't poison your fans.

Magnets

Avery 3270 printable magnet sheets are 8.5x11 and white paper–faced so they can be printed by hand or on inkjet printers. Some people prefer the Staples brand or Print Jet. All are designed for use with the hand-feed slot (see Chapter 3). Lay out your magnets with a 10-up template similar to that used for business cards, or make freestyle shapes and cut them out by hand. These products seem to work best on older, run-of-the-mill inkjet printers rather than newer professional-quality photo printers. Product labels indicate they may not work with every brand of inkjet printer, and opinions vary widely as to whether magnet sheets can be run successfully through laser printers, so try some tests. Rolls of 24x30-inch magnetic sheet paper are also available from art stores and craft outlets for oversize printing by hand.

Thanks to magnets, the refrigerator has become a home gallery and repositionable repository of useful contact information. A selection of professionally made and DIY printed magnets is featured here. Benjamin Davis Brockman's mutant rabbit includes a QR code linked to a website with project details and an animation. *www.benjaminbrockman.com*

Inkjet ink is water-soluble, so if your magnets are going to be out in the rain, overspray with clear spray paint or hairspray once they are dry. This isn't a bad finishing treatment for magnets printed by other processes, such as screenprint with permanent acrylic ink, since it will keep the paper from disintegrating in the rain as well. Printed magnets stick great on car doors, refrigerators, washing machines, and metal light posts. It is remotely possible they could interfere with digital information if stuck next to the magnetic strip of a credit card, so keep magnets away from IDs, plastic cash, and computer equipment.

Magnets, like the other products mentioned, can be ordered to your specifications at online sites, with discounts for orders in large quantities.

Skateboard Decks

Skateboards are a great place to put your own graphics. Blank skateboard decks are available at a number of online suppliers. Decks are generally printed on the bottom with gritty grip tape applied on top. You can customize a blank skateboard deck most easily with hand stenciling, but screenprinting or a linocut can work as well. For screenprinting, burn a photo screen or hand make a screen stencil the size of the flat part of the deck. Make a jig or holder out of wood that accommodates the curves of the nose and tail. Start with a base of plywood a bit longer than the length of the board. Screw short stacks of small 6-inch pieces of 2x2s or 2x4s at each end, set slightly inward from the edge of the base. These will

To screenprint on a skateboard deck, first remove the trucks and then prime the surface with several coats of quality spray primer until the surface is smooth. You can make a jig or holder to accommodate the curve of the nose and tail, or you can simply drape the deck across the arms of an old wooden chair. Find something cheap with flat arms at a secondhand store. *Demonstrated by Lily Parmenter and Samantha Leopold-Sullivan*

Use a few screws to temporarily secure the deck in position with the curved ends hanging over the chair arms. Did we mention not to use your mom's living room furniture?

Instead of hinge clamps, have a friend hold the screen in place while you print. It is recommended that you pull the image twice, in the same direction, without a flood stroke and without lifting up the screen, to really make sure enough ink is deposited. Either permanent acrylic ink or oil-based ink can be used, but be sure to have adequate ventilation if using oil-based products.

If you do squeegee twice, be sure the deck is firmly fastened or it will double print and look "buzzy." Lift the screen promptly and inspect the print. Keep some water (or solvent, if oil-based ink was used) and a rag handy to mop up any mistakes before they dry.

After the print dries, apply a clear acrylic overspray to protect the surface. Bolt the trucks back on so the wheels are securely attached. This artwork is by Drew Mintz. Truth looks good from any direction.

prop up your deck with the curvy bits flopping over, so it can be printed on the flat part of the deck.

Place the deck face down on the rig. Use small pieces of wood, screws, or bolts to secure the deck side to side so it doesn't wiggle around during printing. Unlike rigs for printing on paper, described in Chapter 4, screw the hinge clamps to the wood propping up the deck instead of to the plywood base, so the screen will be secured to print at the top level, and therefore hinged sitting properly on top of the back of the deck. Alternatively, you can drape a board face down across the arms of an old wooden chair. Find something cheap with flat arms at a secondhand store. Use a few screws to temporarily secure the board in position. Instead of hinge clamps, have a friend hold the screen in place while you print.

Using permanent acrylic ink, continue with the screenprint process as described in Chapter 4. It is recommended that you pull the image twice, in the same direction, without a flood stroke to really make sure enough ink is deposited. Be sure the deck is firmly fastened, or it will double print, looking "buzzy." Oil-based enamel ink can be used and is very permanent, but you will need a toxic solvent like mineral spirits or even acetone to clean it out of the screen and off your squeegee. Only do this in a very well-ventilated space, wearing gloves and a respirator.

The pros use curvy screen frames or special rigs to print on curvy surfaces, and if you are handy, you might be able to imagine improvising such a device. Or the pros laminate a preprinted decal to the board. Instead, try printing the nose and tail separately from the flat part of the deck but in the same color and with a slight overlap to create the illusion that it was all printed at once.

Burlap-backed linoleum is fairly flexible and able to follow curved surfaces. Use a jig to secure the board and ink up the linoleum as described in Chapter 2. Print the linoleum face down like a giant flexible stamp, pressing firmly against the wood and working from nose to tail. A second pair of hands to hold up the end of the linoleum while you press it against the wood is a good idea. A third volunteer to lift up the linoleum after you print is even better. The biggest challenge is to not smear the ink. Keep some solvent and a rag handy to mop up any mistakes before they dry. You can always completely clean and dry the board and try again.

Does all this sound daunting? You may want to hire a professional, especially in light of the expense of an individual deck. It's not like printing on paper or even a T-shirt. For about $55, Ship4Free Printing (www.ship4freeprinting.com) offers screenprinting directly on a deck as well as printed heat transfers with no minimum order (known as a "short run") and no setup charge. Order a custom heat-transfer print on a deck or a complete skateboard from places like Sk8 Factory (www.sk8factory.com). Online services for custom laser engraving (fancy woodburning), such as Laser Cutting Shop (www.lasercuttingshop.com), are another option. Download a template and upload your graphics to such sites.

Print on Demand (POD)

Sites such as BoardPusher (www.boardpusher.com) let you select a wooden skateboard deck by size and shape, choose color of grip tape, insert personalized text, and upload your own graphics. They'll even add trucks, wheels, and hardware and ship it to you. They provide handy templates and accept jpeg and png files.

Zazzle will print your designs on a befuddling array of products, including skateboards, T-shirts, mugs, ties, hats, tote bags, key chains, iPad and cellphone cases, speakers, clocks, and even plastic cake toppers. Use a bit of caution as the products are generally cheaply made and the quality of the printing is variable. Zazzle also offers to sell your designs for you at a royalty you set, but as they say in the world of gambling, "the house always wins." No POD company operates as a charitable organization—they are in it to make a lot of money. They save a fortune not hiring professional designers and just give you a small cut.

Still, once you have printed items for sale, it might be good to have more places to sell them than just a card table at a gig. Etsy (www.etsy.com) is the major online player in selling arts and crafts. Unlike eBay, sellers get to customize their Web store's graphics. The charge is 20 cents per item listed, plus a percentage of each transaction. Additional charges include referral fees, PayPal fees, and optional advertising promotions. Shopify (www.shopify.com) charges a flat monthly fee, so you have to consistently sell quite a lot of shirts and posters to make a profit. It is always a good idea to do your homework before committing to any online service. One piece of advice is to set up some kind of web presence yourself—at least a blog—that you control completely and then provide links to selling services from there.

The Pros

The quality of custom hand-printed graphics has risen exponentially in recent years. At the very least, the information presented in this book should prompt you to visit these fine local professional print shops. In addition to their online stores, many have a gallery or salesroom where you can purchase limited-edition posters of fine-art quality. You will be amazed at the beauty, finesse, and variety today's printers can produce.

Perhaps you want to splurge on a large multicolored limited-edition tour poster, which you could sign and sell at concerts. Maybe your cause deserves the attention high-quality protest graphics can draw. Perhaps you need a large run of T-shirts and you're tired of blowing so many when you print badly. If a particular designer works out of one of the hand screenprint shops or custom letterpress facilities in your town, or is available online, and that is just the look you're after, hire him or her. These artists, designers, and printers deserve your support. Trying your hand at printing and hiring a professional are not mutually exclusive. Rather, the one should give you background for an intelligent discussion of the options with the other. You will come prepared to talk to the pros with some vocabulary, choices, and respect for their labor. The finest professional work should inspire your admiration and increase your own aspirations, challenging your skills to make better prints. And if you really have been bitten by the printing bug, see if a print shop whose work you admire needs an intern. Meanwhile, your patronage of independent print shops helps the best practitioners of this medium stay in business and keep producing marvelous examples of printed art.

The Firecracker Press of St. Louis, Missouri, combines antique printing with computer design software. The press hand carves wood blocks and prints them by hand to produce beautiful work like this Mound City Music Fest poster. *www.firecrackerpress.com*

**LIVE MUSIC | SCREEN PRINTING
LETTER PRESS | _SURLY_ BEER
RAFFLE | SILENT AUCTION**

APRIL 7th, 2012

Music by The Lost Wheels · Folk 'n' I

the.bohemianpress.blog

BOHEMIAN PRESS ·

FUNDRAISER

7:30pm - 11:00pm

Located at
LegUp Studio | Casket Arts
681 17th Ave NE · Suite 119
Minneapolis, MN · 55413

POSTER OFFENSIVE № 5

FOLLOW US ON TWITTER!
BE A FAN ON FACEBOOK!

OCT 29 → NOV 07 2010
GALLEY
1224 2ND ST
NORDEAST
MPLS MN

THE SPACE FORMERLY OCCUPIED BY FRANK STONE GALLERY

POSTER OFFENSIVE .COM

OPENING RECEPTION

**FRIDAY
OCT. 29
7:00 PM**

This screaming neon design for Poster Offensive No. 5 even includes a custom font named Rounded Octic. Poster Offensive is a national annual political poster art show promoting peace and democracy. *Artist: Steven Jockisch/www.stevenjockisch.com*

In terms of production values, if you can still read it, you might feel the need to use it. The DIY aesthetic lets you decide. Charm, sweat, and honest labor are evident in this poster from Bohemian Press. Budget time and extra materials if you are the perfectionist type. *Artist: Jeff Nelson/ www.thebohemianpress.blogspot.com*

Opposite: Big Table Studio is a consortium that offers graphic design and printing services to bands. Big Table also acts as a service bureau to other printers, doing everything from making film positives to coating and exposing screens. *Artist: Peet Fetsch/www.bigtablestudio.com*

Ride gravel.
Southern Minnesota

Sticking within a family of tones and using the white of the paper adds to the elegance of this poster promoting bicycling in Minnesota. The artist also designs promotional posters for rock bands. *Artist: Adam Turman/www.adamturman.com*

Mike Davis has a flair for retro 1970s designs with rounded corners and chunky outlines. This five-color screenprint with touches of metallic ink is available from Burlesque of North America's online store (www.burlesquedesign.com). Burlesque will print your poster design to the highest quality standards, even on short notice, for a reasonable fee.

Beautiful use of white, blue-green, and turquoise, along with a dramatic touch of coral red as positive/negative shapes interplay in reflections. The result is reminiscent of nineteenth-century Japanese prints, which often included the supernatural in unexpected settings and a red collector's seal. *Artist: Spunk Design Machine/www.spkdm.com*

Contact information for suppliers, artists, co-ops, and collectives. This list is by no means exhaustive. Hopefully you will seek out resources in your area and find the work of these artists inspiring.

Some of the Artists Featured

Chris Baumler
www.mnartists.org

Rich Black
www.rblack.org

Benjamin Davis Brockman
www.benjaminbrockman.com

Steven Jockisch
www.stevenjockisch.com

Jeff Johnson, Spunk Design Machine
www.spkdm.com

Josh MacPhee
www.justseeds.org/artists

Greg Metz
www.gregmetzartstudio.com

Bill Moran
www.blincpublishing.com

Douglas Padilla
projectlunabrava.tumblr.com

Resources

Broken Crow, muralists Mike Fitzsimmons and John Grider
www.brokencrow.com

Michael Byzewski
www.doomdrips.com

Jennifer Davis
www.jenniferdavisart.com

Chank Diesel
www.chank.com

Peet Fetsch
www.bigtablestudio.com

Eric Fuertes
www.thedumbopress.com

Jeff Gillam
www.designrelated.com/drelatedjeffg

Ruthann Godollei
www.macalester.edu/art/facultystaff

Cole Hoyer-Winfield
www.colehw.com

John Gearhart Pucci
www.linkedin.com/in/johngpucci

Artemio Rodriguez
www.lamanografica.com

Betsabee Romero
www.arte-mexico.com/betsa

Jenny Schmid
www.bikinipressinternational.com

Sean StarWars
www.seanstarwars.com

Colleen Stockmann
www.analogueanatomy.blogspot.com

Xavier Tavera
www.mnartists.org

Adam Turman
www.adamturman.com

David Wyrick
www.mnartists.org

Melanie Yazzie
inkteraction.ning.com

Imin Yeh
www.iminyeh.info

Artist Collectives

The Beehive Collective, Machias, Maine
www.beehivecollective.org

Black Rose Screen Printing Collective, Minneapolis,
 Minnesota
blackroseprintshop@gmail.com

Bohemian Press, Minneapolis, Minnesota
www.thebohemianpress.blogspot.com

Chicago Printmakers Collaborative, Chicago, Illinois
www.chicagoprintmakers.com

Green Door Printmaking Studio, Derby, Derbyshire, UK
www.greendoor-printmaking.co.uk

Iskra Print Collective, Burlington, Vermont
www.iskraprint.com

Justseeds Artists' Cooperative, Pittsburgh, Pennsylvania
www.justseeds.org

Recess Press, Minneapolis, Minnesota
recesspresscollective.com

Leg Up Studio, Minneapolis, Minnesota
legupstudio.com

Living Proof, Minneapolis, Minnesota
wehavelivingproof.wordpress.com

Second State Press, Philadelphia, Pennsylvania
www.secondstatepress.org

Studio Printmakers Collective, Auckland, New Zealand
www.printmakers.co.nz

Studio Rojo, Kansas City, Missouri
www.lauraisaac.com/LauraIsaac/studiorojo.html

Projects

The Art of Downloadable Craft
www.adcsource.com

Occuprint, posters from the worldwide Occupy
 movement
www.occuprint.org

The Irrigate Project, artist-led creative placemaking
 initiative
www.irrigatearts.org

Poster Offensive, poster showcase of political and social
 issues
www.posteroffensive.com

World's Longest Linoleum Print
*www.guinnessworldrecords.com/records-4000/longest-
lino-print*

Hamilton Wood Type Museum
woodtype.org

Arya Pandjalu, Roda Roda Gila mobile stencil
 motorcycle
www.youtube.com/watch?v=GC8ARI7pOjU

Broken Crow, *The Bigger Picture* murals and animation
www.thebiggerpictureproject.net

Cut and Paint, downloadable stencil template designs
www.cutandpaint.org

Kinship of Rivers, connecting the Yangtze and
 Mississippi through art, poetry, and music
www.kinshipofrivers.org

Gary Kachadourian's Cut and City Road
 Construction Set
www.garykachadourian.com

Everyday Poems for City Sidewalk project
publicartstpaul.org/everydaysidewalk/info.html

Print Shops

Aesthetic Apparatus, Minneapolis, Minnesota
www.aestheticapparatus.com

Lunalux Studio, Minneapolis, Minnesota
www.lunalux.com

Burlesque of North America, Minneapolis, Minnesota
www.burlesquedesign.com

Hatch Show Print, Nashville, Tennessee
www.hatchshowprint.com

Drive By Press, New York, New York
www.DriveByPress.com

Big Table Studio, St. Paul, Minnesota
www.bigtablestudio.com

Independent Project Records/Press, Bishop, California
www.independentprojectpress.com

Cannonball Press, Brooklyn, New York
www.cannonballpress.com

Bruno Press, St. Joseph, Minnesota
www.mcbrunopress.com

The Firecracker Press, St. Louis, Missouri
www.firecrackerpress.com

Yee-Haw Industries, Knoxville, Tennessee
www.yeehawindustries.com

Product Suppliers and Service Bureaus

3M—plastic transparencies, tape
www.3m.com

Adobe—graphics software
www.adobe.com

Akua Ink—water-based ink
www.waterbasedinks.com

Apache Open Office—open-source software
www.openoffice.org

Avery—peel-off stickers and labels
www.avery.com

Badge-A-Minute—button-making kits
www.badgeaminit.com

Bay Press Services—graphic art supplies, opaque pens, inkjet toner
www.baypressservices.com

Big Table Studio—design and artwork services, screen equipment services
www.bigtablestudio.com

Chank Fonts!—cool, downloadable open-type fonts, some free
www.chank.com

Daniel Smith Art Supplies—art and printmaking supplies
www.danielsmith.com

Etsy—online retailer
www.etsy.com

French Paper Company—printing paper
www.frenchpaper.com

Gamblin Colors—ink
www.gamblincolors.com

Graphic Chemical & Ink Company—world's largest source of printmaking materials
www.graphicchemical.com

Katz Americas—precut blank coasters
www.katzamericas.com

Krylon—spray paint
www.krylon.com

Lawson Screen & Digital Products—screenprinting supplies
www.estore.ryanrss.com/screenprintingequipment.aspx

McClain's Printmaking Supplies—relief-printing tools, wood
www.imcclains.com

Mohawk Paper—printing paper
www.mohawkconnects.com

Montana Gold—spray paint
www.montana-cans.com

Northwest Graphic Supply Company—screenprinting supplies and equipment
www.nwgraphic.com

Rust-Oleum—spray paint
www.rustoleum.com

Ship4Free Printing—print-on-demand skateboard decks
ship4freeprinting.com

Slam Design—Pickmaster plectrum (guitar pick) cutters
www.slamdesign.co.uk

Smart Set Inc. —digital design services
www.smartset.com

Speedball Art Products—ink and printmaking supplies and equipment
www.speedballart.com

Ulano—manufacturer of screen-making products
www.ulano.com

Uno Hispanic Branding—professional design services
www.unoonline.com

Wet Paint—retailer of art and printmaking supplies
www.wetpaintart.com

Zazzle—print-on-demand site
www.zazzle.com

Index

acetone, 29
Acrobat Reader, 13–14
Adobe Acrobat Pro, 13–14
art centers, 132
art supply stores, 132, 135

barens, 34
brayers. *See* rollers
Bristol paper, 19
brown craft paper, 12, 19
business cards, 138–39
button-making machines, 142
buttons, 142–45

camera chips, 68
cardboard, 10
card readers, 68
carving gouges, 29
cellphone images, 68
ceramic tiles, 122
chalk, 19
charcoal
    linocuts and, 28
    stencils and, 19
circle die cutters, 142
clothesline, 94, 96, 133–34
colleges, 132
community education programs, 132
computer fonts, 10–11
copier paper
    linocuts and, 33
    stamping and, 118
    stencils and, 19
copy centers, 135
copyright, 59
corn oil, 20
cotton organdy, 87
craft paper, 12, 19
crayons, 19

die cutting, 140–42
digital imaging, 68–69
digital printing
    about, 56
    copyright concerns, 59
    digital imaging, 68–69
    finding images, 58–59
    halftones, 69–71
    making the original, 60
    materials for, 58
    paper sizes and weights, 66

performance graphics, 72
photocopy effects, 66–68
photocopying, 62, 64–66
scanner effects, 72
digital projectors, 13–14
drills, 134
drying racks, 94, 134
duct tape, 91

ephemera, 59
EXCO (Experimental College) movement, 132
extension cords, 134

felt markers, 28
frisket, 11–12
Fuertes, Eric, 124

glass
    screenprinting and, 89–90
    stencils and, 12
glue, 82–83
graphic punches, 142

hairspray, 33, 64, 118
hammers, 87, 134
hand presses, 144
hinge clamps, 91–92

inks
    for laser printers, 69
    for linocuts, 33–34, 37
    for screenprinting, 88, 94
    for stamping, 118
    for stencils, 33–34
internet images, 58–59
internet supply sources, 132, 136–37

Japanese mulberry paper
    linocuts and, 33
    stamping and, 118
jigsaws, 134

kerosene, 20
Kinberg, Joshua, 124

laser printers, 69, 134
letterpress printing, 38–40
Lichtenstein, Roy, 70
lighter fluid, 29
lighting, 134
linocuts

about, 26
car as printing press, 42–43
carving, 29–31
cleanup after making, 36–37
drawing images for, 28–29
fabric/T-shirts and, 40
inking, 33–34
letterpress printing, 38–40
materials for, 28
paper for, 33
printing, 34, 36
repairing, 37–38
linoleum
carving, 29–31
repairing for linocuts, 37–38
warming, 31
liquid block out, 82–83

magnets, 145
masking tape
screenprinting and, 82, 91
stamping and, 121
stencils and, 13
mechanic's soap
linocut cleanup and, 37
stenciling cleanup and, 20
workspace set-up and, 133
mineral spirits, 29
miter boxes, 87, 134
Mohawk Superfine paper, 19
Mylar
photo screenprinting and, 83
screenprinting and, 92, 94
stencils and, 11–12, 19

nail polish remover, 29
newsprint
linocuts and, 33
screenprinting and, 91
stencils and, 19

opaque pens, 85
opaque projectors, 13
overspray varnish, 64

page tiling, 13–14
Pandjalu, Arya, 122, 124
papers
for digital printing, 64, 69
for laser printing, 69
for linocuts, 33
for screenprinting, 91
sizes and weights, 66
for stamping, 118
for stenciling, 12, 19
transfer paper, 65, 69
transparency paper, 69, 83–85

photocopiers
effects with, 66–68
positive transparencies and, 83–84
using, 62, 64
photographic emulsion
buying, 88
screenprinting with, 83, 88–89
washout and, 90–91
Photoshop, 68, 70–71, 142
pinback buttons, 142–45
Plexi, 19
polyester monofilament fabric, 87
positive transparencies
about, 83
copy centers and, 135
drawn by hand, 85
making with laser printers, 84–85, 135
making with photocopiers, 83–84
photo screenprinting and, 90
service bureaus and, 86–87, 135–36
power drills, 134
power saws, 134
power washers, 134
premade screens, 88
printed objects, 139–40
printing jigs, 139–40
printing rigs, 91–94
print on demand (POD), 148–49
print shops, 135, 149
pumice bar soap, 20

quartz shop lights, 89–90

razor blades, 10, 20
registration (screenprinting), 91–94
relief printing. See linocutting
rice papers, 118
rollers, 28, 34
roll inking
negative images and, 17–19
for positive images, 19
stamping and, 118–19
troubleshooting, 20
Romero, Bestabee, 124
rotary cutters, 142

saws, 134
scanners
effects with, 72
using, 68
scissors, 134, 142
screenprint fabric, 87
screenprinting
about, 80
coating the screen, 88–89
color blends, 97–98
exposing the screen, 89–90

glue and blockout stencils and, 82–83
making or buying screens, 87–88
making positive transparencies, 83–85
materials for, 82
in multiple colors with multiple screens, 98–99
paper stencils and, 82
photo screenprints, 83
preparing to print, 91–94
printing, 94–96
reclaiming screens, 100
split fountain technique, 97
troubleshooting, 96–97
of T-shirts/fabric, 99–100
using professional positive transparencies, 86–87
washing out the screen, 90–91
screenprint supply houses, 132
screwdrivers, 134
service bureaus
    for transparencies, 86–87, 135–36
    working with, 135
silkscreening. *See* screenprinting
Sines, Ed, 110
skateboards, 146–48
soybean oil solvents, 20
split fountain technique, 97
spray paint
    spray/roll method for negative silhouettes, 17–19
    stenciling fabric/T-shirts and, 19–20
    unclogging, 20
    using, 14, 16–17
    for weatherproofing stickers, 33, 118
squeegees
    buying, 88, 96
    screenprinting and, 94–96
    using with photo emulsion, 88–89
stamping
    about, 110, 112
    cleanup, 119
    finding and making stamps, 112, 114, 118
    on food, 123
    inking, 118
    masking, 121
    materials for, 112
    mobile printing devices, 122, 124–25
    printing, 115, 118–19
    red seal tradition and, 119
    soft surfaces and, 121–22
stamp pads, 118
staple guns, 87, 134
staples, 87
stencil remover liquid, 88
stencils
    about, 8
    with crayons and chalk, 19
    fabric and, 19–20
    making/finding, 10–13
    materials for use with, 10

oversize, 13–14
paper types and, 19
printing with spray paint, 14, 16–17
roll up method for positive images, 19
spray/roll method for negative silhouettes, 17–19
troubleshooting and cleanup, 20
sticker paper
    digital printing and, 64, 69
    linocuts and, 33
    stamping and, 118
    weatherproofing, 33, 64, 118
storage, 134
swivel knives
    stencils and, 10, 12

tabletop presses, 144
temporary tattoos, 145
transfer paper, 65, 69
transparencies
    copy centers and, 135
    drawn by hand, 85
    making with laser printers, 84–85, 135
    making with photocopiers, 83–84
    photo screenprinting and, 83, 90
    service bureaus and, 86–87, 135–36
transparency paper
    laser printers and, 69, 85
    photocopiers and, 83–84
T-shirts
    digital printing and, 69
    linocuts and, 40
    screenprinting and, 99–100
    stamping and, 118
    stencils and, 19–20

universities, 132
utility knives
    linocut carving and, 29, 37
    in workspace, 134
utility sinks, 133

Warhol, Andy, 70
wintergreen oil, 29
woodcutting
    about, 26
    materials for, 29
    See also linocuts
wooden frames, 87
wooden spoons, 34
workspaces, 133–34
Wright, Orville, 110

X-Acto knives, 10

yardsticks, 134
Yeh, Imin, 72
Young, Marcus, 122